ST JO|
LOCKDOWN
DIARIES
2020

How a church in one tiny corner of Wolverhampton coped with the covid-19 pandemic

St Joseph's Church

Merry Hill

Compiled by Tim Eady

Esme Books

Published by Esme Books
100 Bellencroft Gardens
Wolverhampton WV3 8DU
Printed by Book Empire
www.bookempire.co.uk
Unit 7, Lotherton Way, Garforth, Leeds, LS25 2JY

Printed in Great Britain

Although every precaution has been taken in the preparation of this book, the publisher and author assume no responsibility for errors or omissions. Neither is any liability assumed for damages resulting from the use of information contained herein.

ISBN 0-9548726-1-4

To the saints of the Church of St Joseph of Arimathea, Merry Hill, Wolverhampton, who have always brought such enthusiasm, grace, and humour to their faith.

Any profits from this publication will support the continuing work of God's Kingdom in Merry Hill.

Contents

Preface
How it all began

Lockdown: a state of isolation or restricted access instituted as a security measure.

On Monday 16th March, St Joseph's District Church Council met. The coronavirus – covid-19 pandemic was at the top of the agenda. Mid-week meetings, the use of public buildings, any form of social contact were already being discouraged. Images were appearing on our TV screens from other parts of the world of nations being in lockdown: the virus was coming close. We anticipated official announcements at any moment. A decision was taken to close the church hall to all users with immediate effect.

On Sunday 22nd March, Mothering Sunday, instructions were already through that public acts of worship could no longer be held. Some of our members were already beginning to self-isolate. Only a small group was permitted to assemble in order to broadcast our service.

St Joseph's entered the age of online worship. With just the minister and three musicians live on screen, the Butch Broadcasting Company made its debut. Our first 'Facebook Live' service was broadcast. Daffodils and Mothering Sunday cards were blessed, and over the next 24 hours, distributed as widely as possible around the parish, with strict social distancing on doorsteps.

Little did we realise that the next act of worship inside the church would not be held until July 12th, and even then, it would only be a short, said service, with people actively being encouraged not to attend!

On the evening of Monday 23rd March, the Prime Minister appeared on our TV screens and announced that the UK was now officially in lockdown. No schools; no non-essential shops; no entertainment industry, restaurants or pubs; and most definitely no churches. Overnight, our community became a ghost town. Roads were empty; queues appeared outside supermarkets; toilet rolls became precious items. Basic cooking ingredients were hard to find. Hand sanitiser was impossible to obtain.

But in a little corner of England, which will be for ever 'Merry Hill', the congregation of St Joseph's Church settled down to the task in hand – how to be the church in this new environment – not a building, but a community – the community of God's people – seeking, serving, sharing, discovering new ways of being a family, of supporting one another, new ways of 'doing church', and reaching out into the community. Nothing could be organised – meetings weren't allowed – but quite spontaneously, and under the radar, the caring and sharing began to happen.

The commitment of God's people was alive and well. New methods of sharing were quickly, and willingly embraced: Facebook; websites; WhatsApp; Zoom. People who had long fought shy of embracing communication technology, people who had never ever sent an email in their lives before, suddenly discovered the potential of modern communications.

2020 is surely the year when Social Media came of age.

On March 17th, I began to broadcast morning devotions on Facebook live. After 35 years of ordained ministry in which, if I could gather 2 or 3 people to say Morning Prayer, I was doing well, I suddenly discovered that I had an audience. In those heady, early days, our Mothering Sunday service received 2,200 views. Even after three months, daily prayer rarely drops below 50 views. St Joseph's, along with most other churches in our country, was far from finished. Socially distanced – certainly, but spiritually far from distanced. The heart of faith beat strongly. The church was scattered, but rather like those early followers of Jesus in the Acts of the Apostles – as they were persecuted, they were never snuffed out, the church simply spread, and broke out in new places. So now, the church was reaching out in new and hitherto unheard-of ways, and its message was heard, loud and clear.

And as the lockdown continued, it rapidly became apparent that this experience would be a watershed. The church would learn to re-discover itself. And the seed of an idea was hatched. We need to record this lockdown – not with an official history, that is sure to be done by writers and journalists for many years to come, but to record it as it happens, through the eyes of the people to whom it is happening. And as we record our present experiences, what better time than this to look back at the past. What has made St Joseph's the lively, loving community that it is today?

And a new literary genre was created – not really a diary, not a history, not even a straightforward story – but an experience; WhatsApp literature: an immediate, life as it happens, off the top of your head, kind of a literature. A morale building literature; a fellowship enhancing, supportive kind of literature; a literature that's written by everyone and accessible to everyone; a literature in which ideas feed off the ideas of others. And within this WhatsApp literature, there's scope for all kinds of experience: memory, history, mutual support, prayer, encouragement.

And from this humble, WhatsApp beginning, the idea grew larger. Ask people to share their memories, seek out previous ministers – St Joseph's is in an unusual position – its origins are still within living memory. The disciples who built our church are still members of our church. They still talk about building projects, not as remote history, but as real events that they were part of. There will never be a better time than this to get those memories recorded. And in embarking upon this project, we end up with an unofficial history, drawn from the memories of those who have actually shaped the history, as well as recording a commentary upon this present year – 2020 – the year of the lockdown.

St Joseph's lockdown diaries were born.

So welcome to St Joseph's Lockdown Diaries – a unique record of a most unusual year, as seen through the eyes of members, past and present, of St Joseph of Arimathea's Church, Merry Hill, Wolverhampton.

Revd. Tim Eady   September 1st, 2020.

Chapter 1
The Gospel According to WhatsApp

Have you ever wondered why we have three Gospels in the New Testament, which are so remarkably similar that they clearly used the same source material? But yet they each have their own distinctive style, as well as their own original material? And then there is a fourth Gospel which is very evidently telling the same Gospel story, yet is very different, in terms of both style and content, from the other three Gospels. Or why is it that in the Old Testament, the history of the nations of Israel and Judah is clearly documented in the books of Samuel and Kings, but then we turn to the books of Chronicles, and cover the same history, but with a slightly different slant, beginning much earlier in time, and including lots of rather tedious genealogies?

Editing this book has given me an insight into how the Bible was written. In this little capsule from St Joe's Church, we have about 100 different writers. The material has been gathered together from a variety of sources. Some of it is original, written specifically for this publication; some has been gleaned from other publications, written for parish magazines, appeal leaflets, church histories, letters, sermons over the decades. Some is historical; some reflects the lives and interests of members. There is an enormous variety of style – prose, poetry, reflection, history, meditation, humour...

This is not just a book of history. It is a book that future historians can draw upon, and it contains history, but primarily, this is a book of personal memories – the raw material from which history is derived.

And it all began with WhatsApp. So WhatsApp must be our starting point.

It all started with one brick....

Val: In the light of Tim's recent email about the unofficial story of St Jo's, thought you might like this. Here is the wall hanging team.

(Photograph of a team of embroiderers)

            How many can you name?
            Can anyone recall the name of the artist who designed it?
Brenda: Nice one Val!
Tracey: That's lovely, Val. You've hardly changed.

Val:	Ha! Ha! Ha!. It's only because I'm stuck in a rut with my hair style. Everyone else moves with the times and I'm stuck in a 1960s-time warp!
Mary:	Left to right Mary Grainger, next lady to her can't name, Dorothy Turley, Pam Lord in front of Dorothy, Val Plant in front of Pam with daughter Gemma, next to Val Sue Gurney with son Matt, next to Sue Dorothy Robson, Olive Clifford with Nicholas, Gill Ling with Jonathan, not sure of the lady in red behind Gill but may be from the college who helped with the design, next is Evelyn Thompson with white hair, Chris German in front of Evelyn and Sylvia Philips. What an amazing team. I think Beryl Zeal was also involved but not on photo. Can anyone else fill in the blanks?
Tracey:	I don't think it is Mary Grainger, Mary. I think her name was Ann? Friend of Joan Shipway (behind).
Mary:	I stand to be corrected. There was a lady called Ann. I think you are right, Tracey.
Tracey:	Causer has just popped into my head. Yes,
Mary:	you are absolutely right.
Tracey:	She was with us in the choir, I think?
Mary:	Yes, she was. Does look a bit like Mary, but I can see now. Didn't Mary also work on the tapestries if my memory serves me well at my age, ha ha!
Tracey:	I think naming all those others so quickly, your memory is fine. I'm not sure about Mary Grainger.

Val:	Anne Causer and Joan Kirkland are standing on the left next to Dorothy Turley.
Mary:	Yes, it was Joan who I couldn't remember. Thank you, Val.
Val:	The children are Gemma Plant, Matthew Gurney, Ian German and Robin Ling.
Tracey:	Oh yes, of course – Joan Kirkland, not Shipway – a very different lady. Thanks Val.
Val:	Joan and Anne were members of the embroidery guild and did the tricky stitching of faces and thorn bushes. The difficult member to name is Pam Baker in red next to Evelyn – she was a textiles tutor from Old Hall Street who gave us the training and lots of expert advice. The other side of Evelyn is Dorothy Turley's sister in law, Olive, who came from another church to help. Can't remember her surname. Well done everyone. Give yourselves a round of applause. Still can't remember the name of the artist. Have the feeling she was a friend of David Banting and lived on Clee Hill, but not certain. Can anyone help?
Mary:	Thank you, Val. It is good we have this information.
Glennis:	I thought Gill Ling also did.
Val:	Here's one more thing for the archive. This was in the Express and Star.

From the Express and Star April 1990

Putting the final touches to a labour of love... a group of women have completed two wall hangings for their new

Wolverhampton church. The 13 women have spent 200 hours dyeing fabric, 400 hours cutting and 1000 hours sewing to create the hangings for St Joseph's of Arimathea church at Five Ways, Merry Hill. They each took part in a short textile course before setting to work on the decorations which each measure 8ft 6in by 2ft 3in and were designed by a professional artist. Oldest volunteer, 80 year old Evelyn Thomson is pictured with Gill Lang, left, and Pam Baker from the adult college with the finished work. Mrs Ling said, "The hangings will be mounted on the church walls in time for the dedication of the new church on April 7th by the Bishop of Lichfield, the Rt Revd. Keith Sutton.

Val: Yes, you are right, Glennis. Gill also worked at Old Hall Street at the time, which is how Pam Baker got involved.

Glennis: David Banting was the driving force on building our lovely church. He would go on the building site early and pray with the builders. They all enjoyed the morning with them.

Mal: Rachel Harris was the first ever to be baptised in the new church. There were three who were baptised in January 1990. Can visualise the other two but can't remember their names. Rachel was only seven weeks old, but David Banting was about to leave and as she was the youngest, she had the privilege of being first. I think I have a picture but can't find it at the moment. But I do have her baptism card.

Val:	Hi Mal. When you find the photo of Rachel's baptism, please share it. Perhaps we can identify the other families.
	I think the first wedding in the new church was the daughter of Graham, the foreman of the builders who did all the work. We had no minister at the time, so David Banting came back from Oldham to do the honours.
Brenda S:	My memories of St Joe's Wednesday afternoons' Mums and Toddlers.
	Once a month there was a pram service. How grateful I was someone cuddled my baby while I drank a hot cup of tea and ate a biscuit. What a blessing that was! Thank you. What other memories of Mums and Toddlers do people have?
Mary:	Would someone correct me as I am sure you will. I thought the first wedding in our lovely new church was Stella and Derek Hull. Stella was the daughter of Brian Jones – organist at our church. The wedding conducted by David Banting.
Pam:	It was Stella and Derek's 30th wedding anniversary yesterday!! So could well be, Mary.
Mary:	Rev Alex Jack gave Stella away as the wedding had been booked before Brian her father had passed away.
Val:	Thanks Mary. Your memory is better than mine. Do we have any pictures? The group I found to be the biggest blessing was the young Mum's group. We met on a Tuesday afternoon for chat and Bible study, led by Catherine Banting. We all had babies or

young children, so the wonderful Judy Hayward ran a creche for us. Discussing the Bible passages and our faith was life giving. It introduced me to support by the prayers of others. When I look back at the members of that group now, I see what a hot bed it was.

Mal: I belonged to 'young mums' too. It was great that Judy, and if my memory is correct, Hazel Price helped out too. I wasn't a Catherine young mum, but a Linda Hunter.

Val: Yes, Linda took over from Catherine. We carried on until we either went back to work or refused to be called the old wives' group!!!

Cath: That's how I became a member of St Joe's – through mums and toddlers. I loved the Pram Services too Brenda. Then the playgroup with Val Plant and Helen Hills.

Val: I loved leading Playgroup. I took over from Dorothy Robson and Gill Ling in 1987. Gemma was only 12 months, so Catherine and Asha babysat her – took her to Busy Bees at St Phil's. We used what is now the coffee room. It was a little bigger then as the kitchen was in the other end of the building, but it was so dark and crowded. We were full – 25 kiddies and we had a waiting list. When the builders moved in, we moved into the new church lobby. This was before OFSTED and Health and Safety. Moving into the big hall was like heaven!

Caroline: Over 30 years ago, our doorbell rang. The lady at the door said that her church was going to build a new church. They were selling bricks for £1 and would I like to buy one. I did. The caller was Christine German and she lived across the road. She thanked me for being the only person who had so far said yes! A friendship developed and Christine is Godmother to our eldest. Two weeks before lockdown, we met up for lunch and a catch up.

It all started with one brick!

Tracey: When Catherine and David came, their eldest daughter Rachel was the same age as my daughter Jessica, only months old. My Nan, Mrs Bill, began the first St Jo's creche. It was not held in the old church building (as there was no space there). It was held in my Aunt's house and the helpers were Jo and Sam Higgs.

Val: The children in Sunday school brought brick money every week. I think they had a card to colour in. Glennis will know. She ran the little ones group.

Mary: Christine was in Catherine's Bible study group. We had a lovely afternoon of bible study under the apple tree in my garden, with Catherine Banting with Rachel, Val Plant with Helen, me with Andrew. Can't remember who else. Any offers Val?

Val: Will try to remember as many as I can of the mum's group: Dorothy Robson, Phyl Nicholls, Asha Somani, Mal, Rose, Maggie

Mobley, Sue Gurney. Did Sue Tilt and Joy Dale join us?

Tracy: Your Nan was amazing with the creche. My girls were always happy to stay with her at Janet's house.

Mary: I think some people were in the group a bit later, as we did start with only a small number.

Tracey: I can't remember Joy in Young Wives, but Rose will know.

Mal: I remember both of mine taking their brick money to church. There was a wall which they coloured in when they had enough for a brick. It really caught their imagination and was quite competitive as I recall.

Val: My memory plays tricks on me, but I have no photo of the group to check. The group grew quite big and then started to shrink as we drifted off to work.

Mal: A more recent memory when we were introduced to Joe Watts as he gambolled down the aisle with his usual panache and enthusiasm. We were all silenced before a huge round of applause.

Val: Caroline, that's a fantastic story! All because of one brick. We did lots of mad stuff to raise money for the new church. Do you remember doing a sponsored conga around the Merry Hill estate? John Higgs led us with a ghetto blaster on his shoulder!!

Mary: Some of us did a sponsored swim. I can remember Albert Russon and I think Carolyn Harper, including myself. Can anyone fill in the blanks? This was done at Wombourne Leisure Centre.

Val: We collected aluminium cans to sell. It was just as recycling was appearing and only aluminium was worth anything. We had a can crusher on the wall in the kitchen. I remember picking cans from by shops at Warstones and a lady asked me to crawl under her hedge to get the cans that the teenagers had thrown there. It must have been a good couple of years' worth, as I filled two bin bags.

Anybody remember any other stunts?

Rose: Joy started coming to Saint Joseph's when Lizzie joined Rainbows. We pinched her from Beckminster. She wasn't part of young wives' group.

Susan T: Yes Val, I joined the young wives and so did Joy. I remember Linda Hunter led the group, and do you recall the balloon debate on characters in the Bible?

Val: I do remember the balloon debate. Did we all have to be a biblical character. Did we kick Judas out or not?

Susan: I can't remember Val. But I know I was Elijah.

Chapter 2
Way Way Back
Many Centuries
Ago….

The building project of 1988/89 is the one that everyone remembers today, but of course, that is not the beginning of the story. Before the present church building, there was the first brick building – the 'chall', and before that, well let's go back and recollect….

In the Beginning….

In the beginning, there was the parish of St Bartholomew, Penn, which extended over vast swathes of fields and meadows for many miles to the south-west of the small town of Wolverhampton. But the town began to spread. And it came to pass, that by the year 1859, the people of St Bartholomew's parish became too numerous to count, so numerous in fact, that poor old St Bart could no longer cope. And lo - there was a close colleague of Bartholomew – Philip by name – equally zealous in the preaching of God's word – and so the parish of St Philip's was created out of St Bartholomew's, to reach this burgeoning new community. And behold, the population grew yet larger still – too numerous to be supported, even by St Philip's. By 1902, the population of SW Wolverhampton had expanded to such an extent that a mission hut was opened on the corner of New Street and Coalway Road.

And that, is when history began….

In 1929, the Mission Hut became a Mission Church, and moved a few yards further along Coalway Road and was dedicated to St Joseph of Arimathea. In 1955, this wooden building was transformed into a brick building, which in turn was developed and extended until, in 1989, a brand-new St Joseph's Church arose on the site, and was first used for worship on Christmas Eve of that year.

Thirty years have swiftly passed, and today, St Joseph's Church stands at the heart of the community – a people of faith; a people of action; a people with enthusiasm to see God's kingdom extended.

Today, we celebrate all that it means to be St Joseph's Church, Merry Hill.

But who was St Joseph?

There are three Josephs in the Bible.

Joseph Number 1: is one of big names of the Old Testament: a very famous character. Even in our present generation in which biblical literacy is not quite what it used to be, the story of this Joseph continues to be well-known thanks to his amazing technicolour dream coat. This is a story that catches the imagination. This story is important because this Joseph, son of Jacob, is a major figure in the Old Testament. Here is a man who is unjustly accused, betrayed by those who are close to him, left for dead, but who becomes the means of salvation for his family. This foreshadowing of the work of Jesus brings us to the heart of the meaning of redemption.

But he is not the Joseph we are seeking.

Joseph Number 2: is even more famous than his Old Testament namesake. He appears wearing a tea-towel on his head in every children's nativity play that is ever staged. Joseph, of course is the husband of Mary, and famous for not being the father of Jesus. He is described as being a 'righteous man', who agrees to marry Mary despite the unusual circumstances surrounding her pregnancy. Joseph is undoubtedly something of an unsung 'hero' of the biblical story. Matthew tells us that he had plans to break off his engagement with Mary when he learned about her pregnancy, but after a visit from an angel, he agreed to take Mary as his wife, and proved to be a loyal and supportive husband. We have much to thank Joseph for. Although he disappears from the biblical scene quite early in the narrative, we can infer that he was a good father to Jesus (he is still there in the only story we have of Jesus as a 12 year old), acting as a strong male role model, who brought Jesus up in a God-fearing and righteous environment.

But he is not the Joseph we are seeking.

So to **Joseph number 3** – the Joseph in whose honour our church is dedicated: Joseph of Arimathea. This Joseph has just a cameo appearance in the biblical story – appearing in only one scene, albeit the most important scene in the entire story of salvation – and a scene that is repeated in all four gospels. Joseph of Arimathea was a rich man, a member of the Jewish Council, so presumably was present at the trial of Jesus, yet he was a believer in Jesus. Matthew and John both describe him as a disciple of Jesus, whilst Mark and Luke tell us that he was waiting for the Kingdom of God. Joseph was evidently a man of conviction and principle, willing to be known as a friend and supporter of Jesus at a time when the consequences could well have cost him his position, reputation and even his life. Joseph was a God-trusting man who recognised the truth about Jesus.

And it was Joseph of Arimathea who had the confidence and the courage to approach Pontius Pilate to ask for the body of Jesus after the crucifixion. He took Jesus' body and laid it in a nearby tomb. Matthew tells us that the tomb belonged to Joseph himself, presumably ready for the day when he, himself, would need it. It was a new tomb, cut into the side of the rock – quite a feat of engineering. Such was Joseph's respect for Jesus that he was prepared to give it up in favour of Jesus.

We know nothing else for sure about Joseph of Arimathea. We can't even say for certain that he was a member of the early group of disciples. The gospels tell us that the women were 'watching' where they laid Jesus, but it does not say that they were a unified group of believers. However, his devotion to Jesus implies that he become one of the earliest group of believers.

The only other biblical reference that can be interpreted as a link to Joseph of Arimathea, is the prophecy of Isaiah in chapter 53 – part of the suffering servant passage:

'He was assigned a grave with the wicked, and with the rich in his death', (Isaiah 53:9)

Joseph was undoubtedly a rich man, who gave up his expensive tomb out of respect for Jesus.

What else can be said about Joseph of Arimathea? There are no additional historical facts. Anything else written about Joseph moves us into the realm of supposition and legend. There are plenty of apocryphal tales about him. The Gospel of Nicodemus – one of the apocryphal writings of the first century, furnishes greater detail about the tomb, and the burial of Jesus, as well as suggesting that Joseph was amongst the '72' disciples sent out by Jesus in Luke

Beyond this, the story of Joseph of Arimathea descends into the realms of mythology and supposition. The story goes that Joseph was the keeper of the Holy Grail – the chalice used at the Last Supper, and that fleeing persecution, he brought the Holy Grail to Western Europe, finally ending up in Glastonbury, where he preached on Christmas Day, (a mere 250 years before Christmas Day was even invented!), planting his staff into the ground which grew into the Glastonbury thorn – reputed to have flowered on Christmas Day ever since; other legends make him a merchant, who visited England, trading for Cornish tin, coming inland as far as Glastonbury, and perhaps even more unlikely, that he brought Jesus, whilst still a boy, on one of his trips to England, prompting the famous words of William Blake:

> And did those feet in ancient time,
> Walk upon England's mountains green?
> And was the holy lamb of God
> On England's pleasant pastures seen?
> And did the countenance divine,
> Shine forth upon our clouded hills?
> And was Jerusalem builded here
> Among these dark satanic mills?

Interesting thoughts – but surely romantic speculation! Perhaps it is time to move on!

There is enough in the one genuine biblical scene of Joseph of Arimathea to recognise that he was a devout and godly man who was there to minister to Jesus at a time when most other of his followers were too afraid to even show their faces. Joseph is a man worthy of our attention.

Such is the Joseph after whom we have the privilege of naming our church.

But why is St Joseph of Arimathea in Wolverhampton?

The truth is, there is no actual connection between Joseph of Arimathea and Wolverhampton, except for one man – Sir Charles Marston. Sir Charles was a local landowner and businessman, a committed Christian, and a keen archaeologist. In the early 1930s, he donated five acres of land to the parish of Pennfields for a new church to be built at Merry Hill. A wooden church was erected quickly, with a longer-term intention of building a permanent church, with churchyard, for the benefit of the growing local community.

Sadly, the war intervened, and in 1946 the local authority clapped a compulsory purchase order on the entire site, which became in due course, the Warstones Estate. Building took place in the late 40's/early 50's, to be followed by the Merry Hill Tower Blocs in the 1960's. Sir Charles, along with other people, fought this Purchase Order all the way to the House of Lords, but in vain. In the end, only five-eighths of an acre was retained for the purpose of building a church. The original brick building (now the church hall) began in 1954 and was completed in under a year, at a cost of c. £8000 - £1900 of which was raised by children. Their efforts are remembered by the two boards with the 10 Commandments, mounted inside the new church, and still visible in what is now, the hall.

The one condition that Sir Charles put upon his gift of the land was that the church would be dedicated to Joseph of Arimathea. He had become very interested in the archaeological excavations taking place at Glastonbury and was author of an interesting essay on the establishment of the Church in England in the first Christian century. Whilst some of the legends surrounding the visit of Joseph to Glastonbury are fanciful, there is evidence of very early Christian mission in England. Glastonbury is undoubtedly an early Christian site, possibly the first place where the Gospel was preached in England. There is a tradition of early missionaries visiting Britain in the early days of the Roman occupation.

We know for certain that there were Christians in Britain during the Roman occupation. At least one, Alban, was a Roman soldier who gave shelter to a Christian priest who was hiding, for fear of his life. This experience caused Alban himself to accept Christ. Alban took the priest's place, was arrested, refused to renounce his new-found faith and accepted martyrdom on the site that is now St Alban's Cathedral.

So when Sir Charles Marston chose Joseph of Arimathea as the patron saint for our church, he was reflecting his own interest in the archaeological site at Glastonbury as well as his interest in the very earliest days of Christianity in England. His desire was to emphasise the continuity of Christianity in England from these early days to our present time. He has given us the only Anglican Church dedicated to Joseph of Arimathea in the entire UK! As the people of God in our generation, we stand in a long and distinguished tradition!

Chapter 3
How It All Began

The definitive history of the original St Joseph's church was written in 1983 by Don Bannister, a life-long member of the church until he moved away in that year. All later church histories/appeal letters/vision documents – in fact any publication that required some background history to set the scene – has relied heavily upon Don's work. So, it is fitting that our 'Lockdown Diary' should begin with Don's accounts of our origins.

Origins

In the late 19th and 20th century, the Parish of St. Philip, Penn Fields, included the scattered hamlets of Bradmore, Merry Hill, Ryecroft and Bhylls, together with seven farms:- Finchfield, Oxbarn (now Warstones School), Leasowes, Birches Barn, Coalway, Uplands and Beckminster.

A mission room was erected on the corner of New Street/Coalway Road, in June 1902 to hold services, until September 1929, when it was sold for £50.00.

Sir Charles Marston (1867 – 1946), in 1929, gave five acres of land for a new church and graveyard, and later, a parsonage house at Merry Hill. He made the condition that it was to be called – St. Joseph of Arimathea. On this land was built a wooden church at Five Ways, (situated between the present church and the shops.) This was known as the Mission Church, (locally – the wooden hut) and was used until 1955. It was eventually sold to Newcastle, near Craven Arms, for use as the village hall. The sale price was £450.00 and the cheque was paid over on 14th February 1956. An identical building was erected at the rear of the church, used as the scout hut, also used by the church for parties and social functions. The church wardens at this time were Sid Greenslade and John White.

War intervened before the permanent church could be built, and in 1946, the local authority slapped a compulsory purchase order on the entire site, for the building of Warstones Estate in the 1940's and 50's, and the flats in the 1960's. Despite a fight, right up to the House of Lords, only five eighths of an acre was rescued, with very little compensation paid out, and the new brick building was started in 1954, the cost being £8,000. During a four-year period, the Sunday-School children raised almost £2,000. To recognise the effort, two boards were erected in the chancel containing the Ten Commandments in gold lettering on a light green background.

The brick building was dedicated by Stretton Reeves, the Bishop of Lichfield, on Saturday 5th November 1955, with the rural dean – Rev. W. S. Bethway present. Also present were Frank Mansell, the Mayor, and the Mayoress. The churchwardens were Sid Greenslade and Theodore (Theo) Bannister. This was phase one of the project, the second phase being the extension in 1976, on the west side of the church, to include kitchen, toilets and meeting rooms, at a cost of £3,000. Mrs. Prince of Claverley Drive was appointed caretaker in March 1962 at 35 shillings per week. For access to the church, a key could be obtained from Mrs. Curtis, who lived opposite the church.

A significant milestone was achieved in 1978, when St. Joseph's moved in status from a mission church to a District Church, within the Parish of Penn Fields. This gave it a full-time Minister, and a mandate to run it's own affairs. The Rev. Alex Jack was appointed the first Minister-in-charge at this time.

On 5th November 1980, a celebratory weekend marked the 25 years of the "new St. Joseph's". A craft and hobbies weekend was arranged, open to the public, and two former well-loved curates were invited back as preachers for the special weekend. These were Rev. Reg Hoye, and the Rev. Paul Hounsfield.

Looking back, it can be appreciated the dreams of Sir Charles Marston have been achieved, because each step forward was a venture of faith by many people over the years. May this dream continue for many years to come.

(Don Bannister: A History of St Joseph's Church, 1983)

Long, Long Ago….

Geoff Ensor recalls that around 1940, Sunday-School outings were on a canal boat from Castlecroft to the Anchor (past Aldersley), where the children enjoyed a picnic and games, before returning to Castlecroft and the walk back to Merry Hill. It was at this time – 1940 - , that I started in the Sunday-School (so my parents tell me). My memories recall a few events during the 1940's, such as going down the Langley Road to play football on a Saturday morning, on field at Taylor's farm, To save us walking, the curate at the time, Paul Hounsfield took us in his old Ford Poplar car. The bigger boys travelled inside, but I, being the youngest had to travel on the boot with the lid up ….. What safety???

The annual Sunday-School sports were held in the field near the top of Langley Road, where the entrance to Fareham Crescent is now. We had to climb over a stile to get into the field, and I remember the Edwin Nurse, the organist and choirmaster, lived directly opposite. He never married but looked after his elderly mother who lived to "a ripe old age".

Hal Bentley and Sid Greenslade used to organise the sports day and there was great competition to win the book prizes. Oh and the sun always shone. At one time, the sports were held on "the meadow" at the time reached by a double hedged lane from Finchfield Lane. The Meadow has now been built on and is the site of Telford Gardens but used to be a real old-fashioned wildflower meadow.

It was Hal Bentley (a fireman with Wolverhampton fire brigade) who provided a fire-engine bell for St. Joseph's to be rung before the services, to summon the congregation to church. The bell was hung over the door to the wooden church, Philip White and I alternated Sundays for ringing the bell (we alternated pumping the organ). Sadly, one Christmas morning I over enthusiastically pulled the bell rope down, so of all days, no-one heard the bell ring.

The days of the old wooden church were certainly happy days, since it was full, cosy and amply decorated for harvest. Curate Paul Hounsfield had an ambition to form a choir before he left the parish, and this was achieved in 1946, whilst we were still in the wood church. Sitting at the front of the church had many benefits for young choir boys. One was that you were very near to the harvest produce, very often grapes or the occasional apple would "fall into your lap". As choir boys we were often entertained during the service by the church mouse, which would run behind the radiators and round the platform serving as a chancel. Perhaps the most memorable incident for any choir boy was the evening when the local, well respected (nameless) lay preacher was giving his sermon. He said – "the church **must** have foundation!" and thumped hard on the flimsy wooden pulpit, at which his false teeth shot out, were deftly caught and returned so he could continue. Well! Which choir boy wouldn't titter??

I recall many happy hours cutting the church grass with an old push-mower before putting the padlock on the gate and returning the key to Miss Harley at the old cottages.

The old pump-organ was eventually motorised, and Philip and I became redundant, but we had the last laugh. The motor exhaust went through the back wall and had a cover on the end outside. Occasionally the pressure built up and the cover flew off. This meant that Sid Greenslade had to run round the back of the church with his torch and replace the cap. On one occasion this went off with such a bang. We never found the cap and had to use a lid from a jam jar.

My mother did have the misfortune at one evening service to drop her collection, which bounced once on the floor and then landed in the trouser turn-up of the man in front. Well, you can't ask a stranger to look in his turn-up for your collection. Later trousers were made without turn-ups.

During these early days of St. Joseph's, my father – Theo Bannister – always provided the large plaited harvest loaf, a tradition he kept up for many years after we moved into the new brick church.

The Sunday-school became so big around 1950 that the old hose called the Leasowes was used as an overflow for the older children. This house was later knocked down to be replaced with the residential home called Leasowes House, which still exists in Warstones Drive.

I went through the Sunday-School from the age of three, starting in the wooden hut, under the tuition of Harold Buck. Mr. Buck was an amazing character, since he not only served as superintendent of the junior Sunday-School for 25 years, but served in the Sunday School of his pervious church, also for 25 years – a remarkable achievement! I taught for 30 years, acting as superintendent for 17 of those years, but couldn't match Mr. Buck's service.

Over the years we had some enjoyable Sunday-School outings, to Highgate Common, Himley Hall, boat trips on the Staffs and Worcester canal and even a combined parish outing to a school field in Shifnal. We played rounders, tug-of-war and had the inevitable picnic.

A number of social occasions were held from time to time in the wooden church. Mr. Mottram, a member of the parish, used to play his accordion and someone else (I can't remember who), played the musical saw with a violin bow. What a lovely sound it made!

Mary Grainger recalls coming down to St. Joseph's for Saturday Night whist drives around 1950. I remember in the 1940's, someone bringing an old fashioned lantern slide projector with lantern slides, and providing an evening's entertainment of missionary journeys – a forerunner of the slide show. Since television was only just coming in, we were still very much in the days of home-made entertainment.

Later, in the brick church in the mid 1960's, I organised (with lots of help of course), the first summer fayre. Although on a July Saturday, the weather was horrendous and outdoor activities were abandoned early on. Everything took place indoors in the back meeting rooms and a multitude of people turned up, packed like sardines. A good time was had by all, and a grand total of £30 was made towards church funds. Many more of these occasions were held in following years, and fortunately, increased amounts of money were made.

Some of the happiest, and most memorable services held over the years have been the children's Sunday-school Anniversaries. Large numbers of children took part. The boys were encouraged to wear white shirts and grey trousers, and the girls white dresses. The girls were also provided with white headbands. The infants were trained over the years by Mrs. White, Betty Kent, and Pam Teece, whilst I trained the juniors. The pianists for the juniors were Ann Stewart, Harry Stewart, Brian Jones and for many years Kath Taylor. In the days of the wooden hut it took most of the Saturday prior to the services to set up the staging and the long wooden bench seats so that the children could be seen. There were three services each Sunday, morning, afternoon and evening. Many of the parishioners took pride in visiting each other's churches for the anniversary services. The anniversary services continued until I left in 1983.

(Don Bannister: A History of St Joseph's Church, 1983)

A brick church?

There does not seem to be a time in my life when we were not involved with the building of this church of St Joseph's and its growth. My late husband (Sidney) and the late John White were the first wardens, having started in the wooden Mission Church a few years earlier. It was obvious at that time that the people were wanting more services (we only had an evening service), and more contact with the church in this area. It was then (1947) that the Revd. T.P. Hounsfield came to be our first curate-in-charge. He, together with my husband, my sister Lucy and John and Eileen White became involved with thinking of a more permanent building.

Then it was decided to have a whole day of prayer so that we might know God's will – to build or not to build – and God showed us quite plainly what He wanted us to do. So began the great task of raising the money – house to house collecting all over the parish, collecting from Sunday School children etc.

The day our church was dedicated (5th November 1955) was indeed a great day; one for much thanksgiving.
(Elsie Greenslade, written in 1992)

My Spiritual Journey begins

Having spent the first 11+ years of my life 1944 - 1956 living at No 9 Firtree Road, St Joseph's Mission Hall was the destination to which my elder brother Richard and I went each Sunday afternoon for Sunday School. I can recall Donald Bannister (Carolyn Harper's Dad) pumping the organ there whilst someone played it as we sang out the Spiritual choruses of that time. It always seemed then, that the Hall was crammed with children from 4 -12 years of age, arranged around the room in "classes" according to age with up to 12 children in each class. I can still recall that one of my teachers was Ralph Jones who went on to become a Reader across the Parish.

When it came to raising Monies towards the building of the Church (now the Church Hall!), I understand that the Sunday school played a key part, with all of us encouraged to be creative in doing practical tasks both at home and in the community to raise funds and awareness of what was being built. Richard, my elder brother won the prize for raising the most money for the boys..... and the Prize! a full sized Leather Football signed by all the Wolves 1st team at the time!!.... if we had kept the Ball with all those signatures on it, instead of immediately taking it off to Bantock Park to play football! we could no doubt FLOG it for a FORTUNE today!...... signed by the team players who won the 1st Division, now Premier League, 3 times during the 1950's!!!

From memory a Mr and Mrs Buck were a couple who gave themselves unreservedly to the work of the Sunday School and Church at large; even to my infant memory, here were prayer warriors, whose impact will only be known when we see them in Glory. Post War Britain was still subject to rationing, yet another of my memories was of the Christmas Party in the Old Mission Hall for the Sunday School...... fun and games, laughter and pure joy.... and yet where did all those sandwiches, jelly and blancmange come from?.... a touch of feeding of the 5000?.... no doubt many parents and teachers were prepared to go without in order to give us a taste of Heavenly provision.

I may have got this bit wrong but when we celebrated the opening of the new church in 1956, I believe that we

marched down from St Philip's as the Mother church singing with great gusto "Onward Christian Soldiers".....
Rev Caldwell Peers was a great one for open air witness to the truths of the Gospel,

My spiritual journey began in that Old Mission Hall..... yes there were seasons of much backsliding especially from mid-teens to my late twenties... but what a debt is owed to those who sowed the seeds of the Gospel into young hearts like mine. This is the rich legacy on which we continue to build to the Glory of our Risen and Ascended Saviour's name.
(The Revd. Robert Carter)

Long memories

I joined St Joseph's Church Merry Hill in 1958. The Reverend Minister at that time was the Revd. Grundeberg.

In the 1980s, members of St Joseph's Church went by coach to hear Billy Graham when he came to England. We went to Villa Park Stadium to hear him.

I joined the Ladies Guild meeting on a Thursday afternoon led by a Miss Oldbury, and then Mrs Beryl Zeal took over and ran it until 2010. Then it had to close. I joined the Wednesday Circle run by Dianne Davies, which is still running. We had many coach outings which I enjoyed very much. I also served in the church choir and the Ladies Guild choir.
(Joan Jenks)

Carry one another's burdens

In the mid-seventies two people changed my life and way of thinking. They were the Revd Alex Jack, minister of St Joseph's, and Betty Kent, leader of the Sunday School and Wednesday Circle, and also Head of Warstones Infant School, where I was teaching. I had recently started to attend St Joseph's. They welcomed me and invited me to join their home group at Betty's house. Alex and his wife Peggy, who was a doctor, were caring and prayerful. He could often be seen cycling around Merry Hill visiting people in need.

In 1982, when I encountered a very difficult time in my life, they helped me through it, with prayers and understanding. Their support deepened my faith and love of God. When the time came for Alex to move on, our friendship continued, and Wednesday Circle enjoyed coach visits to their home and churches in Burnstone and Little Dunmow in Essex.

Twelve years later, Peggy and Alex received a warm welcome when they returned to Bellencroft Gardens.
(Diane Davies)

Happy Days

When we first got married, I used to go either to St Joe's or St Philip's, depending on what shift Roy was on. Then when we had our first daughter, Liz, a friend said come to the Pram Service on Wednesday afternoon, so from then on, I always came to St Joe's because they were so friendly and welcoming. It was a good get together for all the mums and babies and young children. We sang choruses, hymns, had a reading and a short simple talk then a drink and a biscuit. It was a really good way of introducing children and Mums to God's Word.

Sunday School was held in the afternoon and run by Don Bannister (his wife ran the playgroup). Every year we had a Sunday School Anniversary, where the girls wore white dresses and the boys white shirts and short trousers. They sang choruses and songs for all the congregation. It was a really special event. At Christmas we had the Nativity and the Christingle service – which was the most nerve wracking!! The children paraded in their nativity costumes with lighted candles and sat in front of the communion rails (in the old church there wasn't room to move around), with the tinsel on the angels' heads, and waving Christingles. It was a nightmare for us teachers, trying to keep them all separate.

We became a district church in 1978, and the Revd Alex Jack became District Minister. He was already a curate within the parish.
(De Parrott)

Alex and Peggy remembered....

We were still struggling to stay at "our" church. Then one evening at the front door stood Alex Jack. "We have just moved into No. 100 and we would like to invite you to supper." We didn't realise at the time, but that was the start of 40 years+ at St Joe's.

A relatively short time later, Alex and Peggy left No. 100 (and St Joe's) to take up a new appointment in Little Dunmow, Essex. During Michael and Linda's time the Jacks retired and moved back into Bellencroft Gardens.

Alex previously, had worked in industry, investigating asbestos. His decision to join the Church of England clergy came to him while he was waiting for a train on a platform somewhere! I would suggest that this event was a 'confirmation' rather than a sudden event. Alex wasn't the "sudden" type of person. He was very much the C of E vicar: always robed, robed choir, strict King James Bible, 1662 Prayer Book, Hymns Ancient and Modern; the Minister leads the service, the Minister speaks, the Minister does the Prayers. 8.00am Holy Communion; 11.00am Mattins; 6.30pm Evensong.

Peggy was the "Minister's wife", but as a qualified MD, did some work at a Doctor's Surgery. Both Alex and Peggy were the most gentle, quiet and kind people.

On their return, when Michael Hunter was Minister, things went well as both were of the same mindset. Alex was here through Phil's time as well, and did become a little more "modern", though he did tell Phil, "Nothing any good ever came out of Bristol" (Phil's theological college).

Carl and Alex were much more alike in values, temperament, and Carl was here to support comfort, care and pray for Alex and Peggy as their earthly lives closed.

I am sure both Alex and Peggy heard the words, "Well done, thou good and faithful servant."
(Laurie Edge)

Sickness in God's World

The Revd. Alex Jack, first 'official' Resident Minister at St Joseph's, had a particular interest in the ministry of healing. Here is an article that he wrote.

What is the special role of the Christian faith in the healing of sickness?

Why does sickness happen in the first place in a world which was created by a loving God? It seems clear that sickness and death had no place in God's original creation which He Himself described as good, but they entered into human experience when mankind first sinned against God. This does not mean that the illness of any particular person is caused by sin in his life, but it does mean that they are woven into the tapestry of human life because we are sinful. They are the result of the spoiling of God's creation by man's sin.

God permits illness to come to people, but we do not know why any particular person is ill at any particular time. This aspect of human experience can be used in at least two ways.

a) Satan can use it to cause we humans to hurt each other, and to cause those who are ill to be rebellious against God.
b) God can use it to make people realise their need of Him. We may not understand what God is doing in our lives, but the biblical call is to trust and obey Him (1 Peter 5:6-7).

Jesus healed sick people.

There are numerous examples of this in the Gospels. When Jesus sent out 12 disciples, and later 70 to widen the scope of his ministry, He commanded them to heal the sick. It is important to note that when Jesus began his public ministry, He announced that the Kingdom of God is at hand and said that this was demonstrated by the fact that "the blind receive their sight and the lame walk, lepers are cleansed and the deaf hear, and the dead are raised up and the poor have good news preached to them." (Mark 1:15; Matt 11:5)

Why can Christians expect the Lord's Healing Power to be at work today?

For two reasons:
a) In a spiritual sense, He is with us through the Holy Spirit and the Bible states quite clearly that amongst the gifts He gives to Christians is the power to heal (1 Cor 12:9). We could expect to find amongst a group of Christians certain ones who have that gift.
b) All Christians belong to the Kingdom of Heaven and one piece of evidence for the presence of that Kingdom is the healing of the sick.

The Kingdom will not be revealed in all its glory until Christ returns at the end of the age to judge the living and the dead, when Christians will become like Him, but we should expect to enjoy a foretaste of its great blessings now. God's power is at work in us.

What do we mean by healing?

At first sight the answer seems obvious – a sick person wants to get better, to be set free from the distressing symptoms, whether the cause is physical, psychological, emotional or whatever. But this is healing in a narrow sense, although it certainly is important. We know that in this sense, the Lord does not always heal in response to the faith and prayers of his people. The decision about what is right in ewach case rests entirely with God's sovereign will. He is King of the Kingdom, but the Bible reassures us that in everything God works for good with those who love him. And, we must remember, that even those who were miraculously healed, in this sense, by the Lord Himself, nevertheless at some time later, died. Lazarus was certainly raised from the dead, but just as certainly, died again. Healing, in this sense, even by the Lord, was only temporary.

There is a wider sense of healing. Man is a spiritual being, and therefore the greatest miracle of healing that anyone can experience is that of becoming a Christian by inviting Jesus Christ into his or her heart as Saviour and Lord. This heals the relationship with God, which was shattered by our sin, brings us the free gift of eternal life and is valid for eternity. Ironically almost, death then becomes the gateway into the presence of God and is the supremely healing experience. In this sense it is always God's desire to heal. He longs for people to turn to him in repentance and faith, but of course, He does not compel anyone to do so. (1 Timothy 2:3-6)

God's Healing Power at Work

Even if we think of healing in its narrow sense, i.e. recovery from illness, there are at least three ways in which God's healing power is at work:

a) Recuperative resources of our minds and bodies. God has created us with minds and bodies which have got amazing built-in powers of resistance, resilience and recovery. When we cut ourselves, break a bone, have a headache or infection, we expect to get better, and we usually do. This is such an everyday experience that we take it for granted, but it is God's power at work.

b) The use of medical knowledge which God has enabled men and women to discover and use.

c) Miraculous healing: a direct intervention of His mighty power to bring about results far beyond our normal experience and expectation. This still happens when God decides that it should.

It is important to note that Jesus deals with what He sees to be the person's most important need. When a paralysed man was brought to Jesus on a stretcher, the first thing Jesus said was, 'your sins are forgiven', and only after that arise, take up your bed and walk'. A fellow clergyman was puzzled because a woman who sought the Lord's help on several occasions at healing services for her ulcerated legs showed no improvement. When he mentioned this to her daughter she replied, 'But you don't know what our home life was like… it was hell… I was on the point of leaving… that is what the Lord has been healing.'

What are we doing as a church?

Because, as Christians, we belong to the Kingdom of heaven, and we know that God's power is at work in us and because we know that our Lord certainly has the power to heal any kind of illness and that faith is the means to tap that power, we join in prayer:

We pray with XXXX and anyone else who wishes, to seek God's help in this particular way. We are going to quite deliberately put her life into His hands, as she has already done, and ask Him to pour His healing power into her heart and life and bless her according to her need as it is known to Him.

I am certain that the Lord will answer that prayer in at least one of two ways:
- a) By healing XXXX in the narrow sense of the word, i.e. by curing her illness either immediately or gradually in conjunction with her treatment;
- b) By granting her grace to cope with the situation as He has done so far (2 Cor 12:7-10), and promises to do in the Bible, not in the sense of holding on grimly through each day, but in the sense that the whole of her life and those of her family and friends are enriched by him.

Finally, we can rejoice with XXXX that she has already received healing in its wider sense; she belongs to the Lord and when she does eventually die she is going to be with Him and rejoice in His presence for ever.

Nothing in the whole of creation can separate her from His love in Christ. (Romans 8:39)

(Revd Alex Jack)

Washers, foreign coins, and empty envelopes

My first encounter with St Jo's was in 1972 a few months after we moved to Bellencroft Gardens. I was a young Mum with a six-month-old son. Alex Jack appeared on my doorstep and invited me to join the Wednesday afternoon pram service. My son, Matthew and I enjoyed it very much.

When I started attending Sunday services, I always had a warm welcome. When I went back to work as a primary school teacher, I especially enjoyed the haven of peace and thought-provoking teaching of the 6.30 evening service. Beryl Scorey and I used to share the welcome, reading, collecting and counting the collection duties. This service always gave me the strength to face a hectic week. Now I'm retired I still prefer that type of worship and so go to the 9 o'clock service.

I have been a member of St Jo's for nearly 50 years. In the days of David Banting I organised, did most of the collecting, counting and banking of our Christian Aid Collection. The great British Public was a revelation, donating washers, foreign coins, empty envelopes, nasty comments as well as generous donations and friendly chats.

The other part of my life and St Jo's is as a member of a Home Group. We share wonderful fellowship. As well as studying the Bible we have the friendship, support and confidentiality to share the joys and woes of life.

Though the Church is the people, notable clergy leading us make an enormous difference. The kindness, true Christianity and pastoral care provided by Alex and Peggy Jack, the energy of David Banting, the intelligence and thought-provoking teaching of Michael Hunter, the jolly young family of Phil Cansdale and the spirituality of Carl Rudd. Now we are much blessed by the talents of Tim and Julie Eady.
(Jeni Williams)

Reaching out

When our 4th child was born, we were fortunate that the font had just been donated and our Simon, along with another baby were the first to be baptised in it in 1978. Alex's lovely wife Peggy often looked after Simon and others in the back room while we took part in the service.
(Sue Higgs)

The Key Club

I was a driver for the Key Club and the Ladies Guild. The Key Club was the idea of the Revd. Alex Jack, to enable people who needed help to get to church. It was a monthly meeting and the Leader was Beryl Scorey. Beryl Zeal led the fortnightly Ladies Guild. I really enjoyed the fellowship at these meetings, and I was sorry that they had to close.
(Joan Berry)

The Key Club Prayer

Our loving heavenly Father:
We thank you that Jesus died for us
and is alive and cares for each one of us.
Help us to realise all that this means,
Help us to know that we are never alone.
In pain, He is here to help us bear it.
In fear, He is here to help us face it.
In loneliness, He is here to be our faithful friend.
In life, nothing can separate us from Him.
And when death comes,
the conqueror of the grave is with us.
Oh God, give us the faith of the risen Lord today and
always. Through Jesus Christ our Lord. Amen.

Wednesday Circle

In the early 1970s, two young mothers at St Joseph's, Hazel Mitchell and Brenda Berry decided that although Ladies Guild had been running for some time, there was no group available for young mothers to socialise or have discussions. They began to hold a monthly meeting on Wednesdays in their homes. Unfortunately, they only met for a few months before Hazel's husband changed jobs and they moved to Gnosall, and Brenda became ill. Betty Kent and her neighbour Pat Bannister were sorry to see the meetings close and offered to hold them in their homes. After much discussion a name was chosen, and Wednesday Circle was born.

By the time I joined, they had moved into the church. The meetings were lively with interesting speakers and slide shows; annual meetings with St Philip's Thursday Club, and joining with our Men's Group for Christmas parties.

In 1976, Betty moved to Cumbria and Peggy Jack, our minister's wife took over the leadership. Numbers were growing steadily, and new members were always welcomed.

In 1983, we were sorry to hear that Peggy and Alex were leaving, and so I was asked to lead the group. We continued to play our part in the life of the church and joined in all kinds of activities to raise money towards the building of the new church. By then, it was becoming easier to find speakers. Some evenings were of a more practical nature – making cards, brooches, crackers, marzipan fruits and flower arrangements. Lovely musical evenings were provided by Martin and Kath Fox. Coach outings started earlier and ended late, enabling us to visit Peggy and Alex in Essex, Poet Sunlight on the Wirral, and a tour of he Cotswolds.

Over the years, we have maintained our links with our mission partners, and given support to the Leprosy Mission and Jericho House Refuge Centre. More recently, changes have been made as we adapt to circumstances, so now our meetings are in the afternoons and coach outings have ceased. We all have our memories of past years at Wednesday Circle and we hope to continue to be an outward looking circle, linked together but looking to invite others in and to participate in the life of the church.

We thank God for His goodness and His guidance over the years.
(Diane Davies)

Neil and Helen marry – and make history.

A Wolverhampton church had its first wedding – four years after being licensed to perform marriages. The bride and groom were a couple who first met through the church – then found they both lived in the same road! Biology teacher Dr Neil Ingram (27) wed 25-year-old secretary Miss Helen Bannon at St Joseph's Church, Merry Hill. Dr Ingram first met his bride on a church holiday. The couple both attended the church youth

group and later became engaged. At Saturday's ceremony they were presented with a Bible to commemorate the church's first wedding. By chance, it was Dr Ingram who suggested some years ago that the first couple to be married at St Joseph's should receive a gift. The vicar of St Joseph's, the Revd. David Banting, who performed the ceremony, said he thought many people had been unaware that the church was licensed for marriages. "I am delighted that the first should be two members of our own congregation", he said.
(From the Express and Star August 1984)

A time to celebrate

30 YEARS ON   November 2nd – 5th, 1985.

If your 18th (or 21st) birthday marks your coming of age, then your 30th must surely be a sign of the beginning of the next generation. The present church of St Joseph's will be 30 on November 5th, 1985. We plan a 'Guy Fawkes' birthday party, with an episcopal visit the Sunday before.

Our Foundation Stone of 30 years ago bears the text: "Let us rise up and build" (Nehemiah 2:18). In this celebration, we give thanks to God for a first generation and all who have made it possible. As we look to the future in faith and in commitment to grow, we remember that "unless the Lord builds the house, those who build it labour in vain" (Psalm 127:1). Enjoyment and worship combine together in celebration.

A prayer:

Lord of the church, we praise you that it was your will and pleasure to bring your church into being and that it is now your delight to be her Lord and Sustainer. Thank you for the faithful witness of your people who have worked these last 30 years to establish your church in this place. We ask for grace and zeal for a new generation to press on to know you and to make you known, till all acknowledge you to be their Lord, in the love and power of Jesus. Amen.

Lift high the cross, the love of Christ proclaim,
Till all the world adores his sacred name.
(Parish Letter, 1985)

A Song for St Joe's   New Year 1986
(to the tune of: Lazy, hazy, crazy days of summer)

Roll out those lazy hazy crazy days at St Joe's
Our dedication was in fifty-five.
We're celebrating thirty years of the Lord's goodness,
So now it's roll on two thousand and five.

When our St Joseph made his way from ancient Israel
Arimathea was his hometown.
Some say he got as far as England's Glastonbury:
But we're his sole surviving dedication now.

It's thought St Joseph as a name has Catholic leanings
That would be Joseph from Nazareth.
In fact our name derives in early nineteen twenties

From Sir Charles Marston's love of archaeology.

In preparation for this day of celebration
Some decoration was took in hand.
The thaw in spring had burst a pipe
and spoiled the polish
It has gone in history as St Joe's "Great Flood".

Among our leaders we've got some
who've kissed the Blarney.
Whether they're speaking or writing words.
If it's not David Banting's thirty minutes sermons,
Then it's John Higgs mammoth ten-page bulletins.

David and Catherine have had another baby
Much speculation about the name.
Would it be Joseph, Philip, David or some other?
Of course, it had to be that gospel – he's called MARK.

Now a retired warden sometimes feels a spare part,
But not so Norman, he's struck it rich.
His trips to London, Liverpool, and Bath were sell-outs,
The Finchfield Flier's bound next year for U.S.A.

We are the growing child of mother church St Philip's
We try to play things carefully.
In the first cricket match we won by seen wickets,
This year we honoured them by losing gracefully.

It's always sad to say goodbye to anybody
Like Katie Cornwell or Stella Jones.
Two years ago we thought Gill Westwood gone forever.,
Like a bad penny – from Kenya she's come right back.
(John Higgs)

Chapter 4
Build My Church

If the opening of the first brick church in 1955 marks the beginning of life at St Joseph's as we know it today, then the period of the Revd David Banting's ministry, (1983 – 90) are watershed years. These are the years that everyone who was there remember. These are the years that dominate any conversation about the past. The reason is simple: this is when the second brick church was built, and St Joseph's became the place that we know and love today – long enough ago to be history, but recent enough to still be very much a part of the church's collective memory. Needless to say, these are the years that dominate our Lockdown Diaries.

The Memories of David Banting

I had nearly seven happy years in Merry Hill (August 1983 – February 1990). I was 31, and ridiculously energetic and bumptious. The leadership said that the church was like a ship that had been refurbished and was ready to go but was still in port 'ready to launch out'.

Well, that was like lighting the touch-paper! It was all go as we turned 'Forever amber' into 'green for go', to quote the equally motivated young warden, John Higgs. I recall the moment when we took the end of the Pentecost Service outside the (old) building to conclude by joining hands in a big circle – but then we were aware of a few hands waving down at us from the flats towering above. As we turned to wave back or out, we realised the symbolism of what we were doing – from the reality of our family in Christ (the fellowship of the Spirit) we were reaching out to those outside to welcome them into God's family. The picture of one hand inwards, but the other hand outwards stayed with us. I think that was 1984, the year of the Billy Graham Mission England Crusades, when we took a whole 53 seat coach-load to Villa Park (over half the church), and on the way back committed ourselves to the six-week follow-up course, which in turn laid the foundation for and turned into our first Home Groups. It was at that time that the great processional hymn 'Lift high the cross' became a bit of an anthem – lift high the cross over St Joe's and over Merry Hill, the inspiration behind the cross that surmounts the new church building.

Quite apart from the birth of our first child (Rachel) within weeks of our arrival, John Higgs (he was the Hermes to the Zeus of other older, quieter warden, Norman Walthew – see Acts 14:12) described that first year as a 'year of firsts'. I remember we started a creche – and all because of the amazing Mrs Bill (Tracey Bennett's grandma). Mrs Bill was looking after Tracey's first born, Jessica, born about six weeks before our Rachel, during Sunday morning services. A few weeks after Rachel was born, she offered to look after her too at Tracey's house. A few weeks later, I suggested she might like to look after them in church – and the creche was born. It helped see most of our early growth in families – Mrs Bill at the very heart of it. Nothing phased her in littl'uns (either end) and she made a point of never having to call any parents out. She ruled the roost with an iron will and a heart of love. I've always thought the heart of any creche is a seasoned granny to act as anchor every week, a Mrs Bill. She handed over eventually to Hazel Hughes who ran it with equal verve, creating a giant growing sun-flower – a petal for each child (with their birthday written in) and a polka dot on the petal for every attendance. Yes, happy days…. I'm not surprised we decided in 1985 to celebrate the 30th birthday of St Joe's with the sense of something more to come.

Baptisms invariably grew in number (I was indebted to John Stott's article on 'the evangelical doctrine of baptism' for my approach and practice), but so dramatically, did funerals. I had grandly said to the Vicar of the parish that, rather than divvying out hatch/match/dispatch occasions amongst the three clergy of the parish, I would take all such occasions that came out of the district, i.e. some 10,000 out of the parish of 23,000. By the end of the first six months I did not know what had hit me – I had taken 50 funerals and was swamped! My all-time record was nine in a fortnight. In one sense I got so angry doing what seemed at times like nothing else… until I suddenly realised that everyone seemed to know that I was the local minister, and that I was OK (I had gained an unseen congregation from all the funeral congregations, all drawn, of course, from the local neighbourhood). The Warstones Estate was built straight after the war and 40 years later large numbers were beginning to die off. Funerals continued at a rate of 80 – 100 a year most of the time I was there, but that too was a great point of growth.

There are so many other names that float back into focus: Bryan Jones the organist, a big man who you sensed you needed to keep on the right side of, but a spiritual giant (in whose memory the organ for the new building was donated by TarMac, his company); or his daughter, Stella, also wonderfully musical (we had concerts and put on musicals) we ran the CYFA group till Jimmy Orotayo came as a 'Ministry Trainee' (before they were called anything like that) – she's down in Lewes, Sussex now with husband Derek, now retired and their now married children; gentleman Gordon Rostance, the ex-Mayor's Secretary, our Treasurer and (after an extraordinary dream) the Chair of our Buildings Committee; a later Warden, Brian Templar, who was plucked from being just an 8 o'clocker, to be Warden, and whose indignant question (when one too many pieces of tat was brought to the church), 'Do we have a hand-me-down God?', led to a banning of Jumble Sales as a means of 'raising money' – and almost immediately to a rise in giving, and our commitment in the new buildings to 'only the best for God'; Glennis Potts, Pam Teece, De Parrott, Steve Robson, the Lord family etc. etc. – such a wonderful family and great team, so forgiving of me and my enthusiasms and so supportive of me and my family as we got going.

Of course, my final few years were dominated by the Building Project, our great 'Venture of Faith' (the title of Bishop Michael Baughen's inspirational book on Moses and of his memorable weekend with us for the foundation stone laying).

It was such a privilege to build a new church when so many were beginning to close. It's the people that stand out: Gordon Rostance's dream and his masterly skills as the project chairman. Archdeacon 'Tricky Dicky' (Richard Ninis) pulling a grant of £150,000 out of the bag (about 40% of the total); the secular site-foreman Graham Copper's growing sense of awe at building... a church (and not just shops and offices) – we still exchange Christmas cards; the local Baptist Minister's astonishment that we were putting a baptistry at the heart of it all; the utter magic of our first service on Christmas Eve – and, to Graham's absolute mortification, it leaked in the top left hand corner – it was a gutter-joint leaking, which he had fixed the next day – Christmas Day! We knew we were venturing in faith and building for the next generation.

I left within six weeks of that first service, well before the Dedication set for April 7th – it's just gone another 30 years then for the new St Joe's. Another very different memory continues to humble me. The Diocesan Bishop was the lovely evangelical, Keith Sutton. In 1988, as the project began, I gave him our Motto Card for the year – Luke 1:37-38. It was rather forward of me and 'in your face' – the card was bright red and the Minister young and a bit bumptious. He received it with his customary good humour. When the new building was complete, almost the last thing I did before I left was to craft the Dedication Service, which I thought would help the Vicar of the parish who played very little part in the project. I had secured Bishop Keith and gathered material from the diocese and elsewhere as well as including particular touches distinctive to St Joe's experience. I left it with the vicar and left for Oldham. But the vicar was very upset, and so, subsequently was I – after all the trouble I had taken and indeed been through! From my new home I rang Bishop Keith and poured my heart out, all the disappointment, frustration and angst. He just listened on the phone. Eventually he said, 'You're a Greek scholar, aren't you? You recall the word used in Acts 15:39 when Paul and Barnabas fell out – it is usually translated 'sharp disagreement'. But that is perhaps an understatement. The word is paroxusmos, from which we get our word 'paroxysm'. Paul and Barnabas had an almighty bust-up – but you know what, what God made of it – instead of one mission, two missions went forward! God is not wrong-footed by our messing up or falling out. You get on with the mission of God in Chadderton and let the Vicar get on with the mission of God in Pennfields – two missions going ahead.' I was duly humbled and well pastored.

Within three months, I had returned three times – for Bryan Jones' funeral; for the dedication service, when I sat on the front row enjoying the occasion but having no part in it; and for Stella Jones wedding. I had visited Bryan in hospital with cancer during my last week – we both knew we would not see each other again. I read and prayed. As I turned to go, I said (looking around the swanky new BUPA hospital) 'Well Bryan, you're in good hands.' He looked me back straight in the eye and said, 'Yes, I know I am in good hands.' And I knew at once that he meant the Lord's hands and that there, he was eternally safe. John 10:27-30 have been my go-to verses at the bedside. Stella and Derek's wedding is also memorable – for two reasons: it was very much in the shadow of her Dad's death, but a sense of his love, and also it was the first and almost only wedding where the couple have learned their vows and spoke them direct to each other with no 'Vicar's autocue'.

There is a PS to kindly Bishop Keith. Over ten years later I met him at General Synod (I was first elected in 2000). I had heard that his dear wife Jeanie was deep into Alzheimer's and no longer recognised him, though he continued his episcopal ministry. He told me then, when it was confirmed that she had dementia, he came across behind his clock on the mantelpiece a shiny bright red card with the words, 'With God nothing will be impossible… may it be to me according to his word'. He said that those were the words he needed to hear, and that he came back to them often. It remained prominent on the mantelpiece.

Two unrelated memories somehow capture the sheer fun and adventure. One was a Youth Group CYFA – I am a pyromaniac, so every November an excuse for a bonfire. A bonfire made for a great CYFA social. That evening, while I was doing some washing up after the toffee-apples and toasted marsh mallows by the fire, I saw out of the window that the boys had raided some of the bags of left-over clothes from a jumble sale (sic!). They had thrown many of the clothes on the fire but were wearing some older ladies' underwear (!) on their heads to cavort around like banshees. As I came out, a fire engine came screaming up – two officers rushed up with a hose and unceremoniously doused the fire and started tearing strips off the lads. Someone from the flats had seen some 'hooligans' lighting a fire at the church and rung the emergency services. The officers were clearly annoyed. 'Who's in charge here?', they demanded to know. When the kids pointed at me and said I was the minister, theirs gasps were flabbered. Of course, the fire was well and truly doused – and the half-burnt clothes were soaked and took days to dry. If they had waited another 10 minutes, the clothes would all have been burned and disappeared. As it was, the bonfire site was left a mess and a scar on the green.

The other was an historical anniversary – also involving fire. The year was 1988, and various anniversaries were picked up by the Reformation Society – the 400th of the Armada and Protestant England's victory, and the 300th of the Glorious Revolution when William of Orange's arrival ensured the continuity of the Protestant English monarchy. We were all encouraged to light beacons in memory and give thanks for the preservation of the faith. Completely unnecessary in one way and offscript, but we had fun with history and faith…. And fire! And it seemed to add a bit more to the adventure.

As I look back at my first real responsibility for a local church under God (but still not a vicar of a parish), I realise just how much I wanted the faith and fellowship of Christ to be a memorable and joyful adventure. I have always enjoyed the song 'The Lord of the Dance', more than I probably should have, but it always suggested that the Lord Himself was leading his people 'a merry dance'. The Lord certainly blessed us as we 'launched out', and His Word did its work and grew the church.
(Revd. Canon David Banting)

The PCC gets involved

A Statement to be received by the PCC, October 30th, 1985

A District Church

St Joseph's became a District Church in 1978 and was provided with a constitution. That has proved to be both a pioneering document, (devised from scratch to fit the parish circumstances), and something of a time-bomb, in that it gave a very high degree of autonomy which God in His timing and working through a sequence of leaders has seen fit to realise in large measure now. At the time it provided for a real separate identity for St Joseph's and an appropriate continuity in ministry. However, the full implications remained veiled or dormant for a while.

A Sequence in Leaders

Alex Jack was experienced in the parish and on the one hand provided an essential stabilising element while we found our feet and muscle: he was a very clear-headed administrator. On the other hand, he asserted strongly that he was now employed by the Bishop rather than by the Vicar. His whole policy was a very successful balance of the links between us, the Parish and the Diocese….
David Banting came direct to St Joseph's, not "down from" the parish…. under the aegis of a "new" vicar….
Between these changes came our own interregnum (April – August 1983), in which lay leadership assumed a new importance. The Wardens' role underwent a speedy and

dramatic evolution with little assistance from the parish. We were trusted to conduct our own affairs with near-total freedom….

As the DCC got established, it developed from considering merely practical issues to taking responsibility for the spiritual tone and direction of St Jo's. It is now very much a leadership team in training and alive to the task of bringing about the Lord's business in the Merry Hill area.

A Distinct St Joseph's Identity

With confidence came a realisation that the methods of St Philip's were not always the right ones for us – e.g. financial approaches to the congregation, communication, baptism preparation, missionary giving – and thence a growing awareness of our separate identity and that of community, together with our necessary response to that. The flats and the new estate present a different challenge: their orientation to young families and fluid composition are different from the more static and longer-established area which the Parish Church serves. Our central site and being the only church of any denomination in the area make us especially image conscious. In May 1981, St Joseph's was licensed for weddings and given a clearly demarcated pastoral area and catchment area – down Warstones Road to the Coalway Road roundabout and then round the back through Langley Gardens to run out down Coppice Road (c.3,300 homes; population 9,000). As weddings, funerals and baptisms become increasingly referred to St Joseph's directly and automatically, the community begins to perceive us in a different and more conscious way.

The Present Position and Future Hopes

So we find ourselves in a situation where our buildings are inadequate for present needs, and restrictive of future growth; where we serve a population and area not far short of that of the rest of the parish (reflected in our proportion of the Electoral Roll); where our annual budget has grown out of all proportion.... Even to the point of being able to assist our erstwhile parent with her deficit two years ago; where we no longer need external support, other than in prayer; where home groups are well established and are intended to form the core of our pastoral care; where the workload for the Minister for the specific needs of St Joseph's is well past 100%; and where we are able to sustain ventures such as church weekends away and, conceivably, our own Area Mission.

A Growing Family – the Unavoidable Picture

As a former daughter church, the comparison with human families is perhaps trite, but inevitable. Before 1978 we were the dependent child.
(PCC Discussion Document, 1985)

'With God nothing is impossible'
(Motto for 1988: The Parish of Penn Fields)

In the Autumn of 1987, the church ventured away to Shallowford House for a weekend of peaceful recollection. There was to be no study subject, simply a time to devote to God and listen to Him. We were asked to consider the statement: 'God knows what he is doing'.

God said 'Build my Church' three times to three different people. The first was to Gordon Rostance: who was a quiet Godly, smart man, who rarely said anything but when he did people listened. God chose wisely. God then spoke to two ladies from the church. On each occasion the minister at the time suggested that they tell no-one.

Eventually it became clear to everyone that our church was not adequate in so many ways. A committee was formed, and we were directed to Michael Baughen's book 'Moses and the Venture of Faith'. We soon discovered we could not have chosen better. Just a couple of years later Michael Baughen, as the Bishop of Chester, laid the foundation stone for our new church with the inscription:

'with God nothing is impossible' Luke 1 v 37

To someone on the outside it must have seemed that God's people would let Him down. They didn't! The church was built and paid for by His people here in Merry Hill. The DCC minutes recorded that the architect was instructed to design a church for double the congregation. It was going to cost a great deal of money, but we were encouraged by words in a sermon by

Michael Baughen who said, 'no thermometer outside church simply pledges from the heart'.

I remember visiting St Michael's Catholic Church to experience a round church. The priest there wanted to know how we would pay for it. I said that we were going to do it out of our own pockets. He responded that we would never do it, and that he would not get the money out of his congregation. It is to my eternal embarrassment that the DCC did not communicate a suitable reply. The Rev David Banting asked for pledges. The first and probably one of the biggest was from his father. A few grants were received but the church was built mainly thanks to the pledges from the congregation and of course, the children were involved by bringing brick money each week.

Our church was built for God, His people and the local community.
(Brian Templar)

The Vision Grows

Gordon Rostance was one of the key players of this period. Whilst waking one morning in 1985, he heard a "very loud, deep and very clear voice say, "Build my Church". This led to the founding of a buildings committee, who worked with the church, the diocese and the architects to prepare ambitious plans and estimates for what would be a new church built at the side of the then church. It would accommodate over 200 worshippers in an attractive and flexible space, and would free up the 'old church' to be a resource for the church and community alike.

During this period, the church was encouraged in particular by the biblical figure of Moses, who showed great faith in a great God and acted on that. Given the scale of the project, igt would not have been difficult to shy away from the challenge, but instead the congregation stepped out in faith and trust.
(from Onwards and Upwards, written in 2005)

Document prepared for the Parish Joint Standing Committee, July 1987.

There had been rumblings for some time about the chaotic situation for storage....
in addition to the needs for storage, the creche, and Pathfinders, the focus grew:

Space
> in the church – no welcome or "mingling" area for people, fellowship, publicity.
> Wrong shape, too narrow; increasingly too small.
> Seating for 125, on occasion treble that number has been shoe-horned in.
> Sanctuary is undignifiedly small, and the Communion rail only takes 6.

Facilities
> Kitchen primitive, tiny, isolated.

Appearance

throughout, second-hand, dowdy, even "shoddy"
Building not recognised as a church, no external witness

Growth

the church is usually 80% full, but the congregation followed the DCC's clear lead and commitment to work to bring people to Christ and to see the congregation double in five years. Growth, actual and planned, suggested a larger church.

The Project comes clearer and closer

An architect, (George Sidebotham) was engaged in July 1986 and produced a plan for a new church to seat 250. Cost – a staggering £370,000! Further reflection has issued in a request to the architect to endeavour to keep the cost down to £250,000….. St Joseph's have already received a very considerable encouragement fron the diocese.

The Master Plan

For a cost of £250,000, the architect is now finalising his draft design for:
A new church on the grass area behind the existing church, to seat 250 in a square design.
The existing church to become a large hall.
The kitchen to be enlarged, upgraded and re-sited

Meanwhile, back amongst the congregation....

Whilst the plans went through the PCC, the Diocese and the local Planning Authority, the members of St Joe's began to mobilise. £250,000 to raise? With volunteers like these.... no problem!

Raising money for the new church Late 80s.

Strawberry Teas

For at least two, possibly three years running, we had a Strawberry Tea at my house to raise money for building our new church. They were held on a Saturday in June or July and everyone was invited. My daughter baked at least 300 scones one year which all seemed to get eaten so either everyone was very greedy, or we had loads of visitors!

For a set sum of money, you could have two scones, jam, cream and strawberries plus a cup of tea or coffee. Other people brought cakes which we put up for sale and had a raffle too one year. I remember my daughter making two patchwork cushions and Joyce Hill making a beautiful chocolate cake which we raffled off.

Included in the afternoon was a guided tour of my husband's pride and joy – our big garden – full of flowers and vegetables. This was usually undertaken by one of the grandchildren who took great pleasure in showing people all the places they played in (and probably all the places they shouldn't have).

All in all, they were enjoyable days and of course, the weather was always beautiful.
(Olive Clifford)

I wore my wife's swimming costume

After 13 years at St Aidan's, I came to St Joseph's in 1985. I became a member of the church committee and at my very first meeting Revd. David Banting said "we need a new secretary. What about you Albert? You must be used to pushing bits of paper around."

Much to my surprise, I said "OK" – a decision I was later to regret.

I already knew Gordon Rostance, a lovely man and a church elder, who it was reputed had heard God say, "build my church". Discussions were already afoot, and the decision was made to build a new church. Gordon and myself knew that a lot of money would be needed to pay off the loan for the building, so I picked him up one afternoon every week and we drove to Wolverhampton Central Library and there on the top floor reference library we discovered a gigantic book full of organisations that gave money for causes that interested them. There were many diverse reasons why they would or would not help people in applying, so Gordon and myself gradually worked through the book and made notes of those we thought might help.

We passed the details to David Banting, who wrote to them. In the course of time we obtained several thousands of pounds.

We also had a leaflet listing all the things we wanted to do. Several of us delivered these, knocking on every door in the parish – a formidable task. Events took place to promote awareness of the new building. I and several others went round the parish dancing a 'Conga'. John Higgs carried a portable radio. Wow! Our legs were sure aching after that.

One gentle activity that everyone joined in was a sponsored walk from the church through the Warstones Estate. I wore my wife's swimming costume, and as we reached the end of the field, there was a small boy climbing a tree. He stared at me, then nearly fell down and shouted, "are you a man or a woman?" People took push chairs, and many wore fancy dress.

A memorable occasion was the laying of the foundation stone. The Bishop of Chester had taken great interest in the new church, and. Came to officiate at the ceremony, as we clustered among the paraphernalia of the building.

As the new building neared completion, and opening day approached, David Banting sent letters to all those who it was thought might want to attend. As secretary, it was my job to write to them and enclose the tickets (which were limited to about 300). The mere addressing of envelopes was a formidable task, and I was glad when that was all over and everything went well on the day.

We still had a huge amount to pay off on the loan. Roger Nicholls, Beryl Scorey and I formed a Development Group. Beryl thought of many good ideas but pushed Roger and myself into organising these events, whilst she organised tickets, programmes, leaflets and posters and cajoling people to send refreshments. Penn Choral Society were well known and gave us two concerts. The church was packed out. St Andrew's Church, Sedgley had a fantastic choir who also came. These concerts brought in thousands of pounds.

We also had our own show or two and it was surprising what talent we had. Roger made an excellent compere and enough acts to fill the entire evening. I sang a coiple of George Formby songs. Revd. Alex Jack did his Albert and the Lion act. Little Jonathan Harper was 5 or 6 years old and just learning the violin. He was very brave, sat in front of us all and played beautifully.

Oher people worked in many other ways towards the same goal. Many events were held in the church grounds including a balloon competition. One or two balloons even reached the continent. It was always enjoyable on a hot summer's afternoon, and the new kitchen did a roaring trade.
(Alfred Russon)

Express and Star April 1988

A Wolverhampton vicar is swapping his cassock and prayer book for running shoes – to raise funds for a new £400,000 church project.

The Revd David Banting, Minister of St. Joseph's in Merry Hill is planning to run his first ever marathon on Sunday. He hopes to raise £1000 towards a new church which will replace the current building. Development work on the scheme will begin in September. The Rev Banting said, "I plan to run three and a half circuits of our church district. Although I dislike long distance running intensely, I am determined to complete the distance. It will be the first time I have ever run a marathon and I have been in training for the last few weeks."
(The Express and Star)

And so, to building

Revd David Banting was the instigator of having a brand-new church and using the old church as the hall (which it had always intended to be). Gordon Rostance, one of our church members, had a vision one night of God telling him to build the church. Henceforth everyone got behind David and we started to raise money for the building. I made money boxes for the Sunday School children to collect small change in, which is surprising how it mounts up. They were ordinary plastic butter boxes with a slit on the top and pasted on the sides "Build the Church" and "Buy a Brick", and on the top,

"Thank you". In fact, I still have mine in which I collect small change for one of our Wednesday Circle charities.

People and Sunday School made varying designs for the wall hangings, but an artist from Stourbridge or Worcester way did the designs for the ones that are hanging.
A group of keen sewing ladies got together and under the guidance of Gill Ling (Olive Clifford's daughter), with the help of a lady from the Adult institute produced the beautiful hangings. Some of the material was hand dyed to produce the colour needed, then it cut into the appropriate shapes and sewn by hand onto the background – similar way of doing a collage. Joan Kertland and her sister Ann Causer embroidered the faces and any other little bits. All the ladies' names are on the back of the hangings.

Some of the other hangings were done by Olive Lowndes and Dorothy Turley, who also did the tapestry of "Christ at the door'.

All the kneelers were made by ladies and their friends who were keen crafters.

The vision and all the work was our way of thanking God for all that He gives and gave us, in building the new church.
(De Parrott)

David Banting takes up the story *(extract from the Pennfields Parish Magazine, c. 1987)*:

The Opportunity of a lifetime

In the Middle Ages, it was actually quite common to be involved in building a new church. Even a hundred years ago, many of our forbears had the chance to build for the glory of God. But now it is rare.

However, in our generation, we are now being given the special opportunity and privilege to build a church and to create a new church centre for Merry Hill and the surrounding community. This is our rare chance to work so visibly for the glory of God in our own neighbourhood. The whole area is, after all, still a comparatively new community, being developed and built up since the last war. It is good that Christian witness should have so clear a focus in our midst.

But of course, at a cost.... at the cost of great sacrifice to individuals and to church.
(David Banting)

By the end of October 1988, there was no turning back. A parish weekend was held, the Bishop of Chester invited, and the Foundation Stone for the new church was laid.

Extract from the Service of Thanksgiving and Dedication to mark the laying of the Foundation Stone to a new church centre, by the Rt Revd Michael Baughen, Bishop of Chester. (October 29th, 1988)

Our principle offering today is not for ourselves, but for the parish church of St Philip's, who are today holding a Day of Prayer and Giving towards a target of £12,000 for a new heating system to be installed as from Monday after 15 months of cold....

Any children present are invited to take a brick from the lobby with them as they go out – they will be able to "sign" them personally and know that their brick will be built into the whole.

The Bishop will officially lay the foundation stone and lead us in prayer. The inscription contains part of the parish motto text for 1988: 'With God nothing will be impossible" (Luke 1:37). Before we return to the church, we'll wave to the "thousand eyes" in the flats.

Act of Dedication for God's People

Bishop: Do you own and acknowledge Jesus as your Lord and Saviour?

People:	WE DO.
Bishop:	Will you seek to serve our Lord Jesus Christ and his interests faithfully, sacrificially, cheerfully, and with zeal?
People:	WE WILL
Bishop:	In all your labours and priorities, will you be faithful in prayer, obedient to the Word of God, dependent on the Spirit of God, and seek to demonstrate the love of God?
People:	WE WILL
Bishop:	Will you reach out and welcome others as Christ has reached out to you? Will you in every way strive to promote the work of the Gospel, and the kingdom of God and his glory?
People:	WE WILL
Bishop:	Jesus, Master, you know us by name. We bring you ourselves, our souls, our bodies, our strength and weakness, the work we have done, the sins we have committed. But the Kingdom is Yours….
People:	….and the power and the glory.
Bishop:	We bring you the people and the things we love, our hopes and fears, our temptations and ambitions. But the Kingdom is yours….
People:	…. and the power and the glory.
Bishop:	We bring you this day of small beginnings, with all its celebration and challenge, its hope and promise, its opportunities for your glory. For the Kingdom is Yours….
People:	….and the power and the glory.
Bishop:	Bless all we have set our hands and hearts to do, our homes, our families, our community, our church. Lord God our

Creator and Provider, we pledge ourselves afresh to work and prayer, to giving our resources, to proclaiming the gospel; we pray that you will guard our getting, direct our spending, and bless our giving. For the Kingdom is Yours….

People: …. and the power and the glory, for ever and ever. Amen.

We're on the Way!

Wolverhampton churchgoers set their sights on higher things when they laid the foundation stone of their new £350,000 building. They hope to see it complete, with spire, by Christmas of next year.

But first the congregation of St Joseph of Arimathea, in Merry Hill, still have to raise £80,000. To inspire them, they invited the Bishop of Chester, the Rt Revd Michael Baughen, to lay the foundation stone. His book, about two building projects, gave them hope when they came across it two years ago, said the Rev David Banting, minister of St Joseph's.

"It was a great privilege for us to bring him out of his diocese to our dedication service," Mr Banting added.

About 170 people attended the service for the start of the building which will seat 240. It is planned to turn the old church, which is now too small, into a community centre.
(*The Express and Star, October 31st, 1988*)

And out to the parish, (1989):

I have served as the minister of the District Church of St Joseph of Arimathea for six years. In that time, I have had the privilege of meeting a great number of you personally, in times of joy and celebration or of sadness and difficulty, at new beginnings or simply around the place. Thank you for every opportunity to be a teacher and a pastor.

I would now like to ask for your help in our Development Project, in our venture of faith.

The people of St. Joseph's believe that we have been given a once in a lifetime opportunity to build a new church to the glory of God. The building began last October and is now rising rapidly, as no doubt you will have seen. The new church should be ready for this Christmas and the church centre by about Easter 1990. I consider the project a supreme privilege. But we need your help.

St Jo's is part of the large parish of St Philip's and was built over 30 years ago to serve this end or District of the parish. This "District" now has a population approaching 10,000 and includes Merry Hill and large parts of Warstones and Finchfield.

The foundation stone for the new church was laid on Saturday October 29th, 1988, by the Bishop of Chester, the Rt Revd Michael Baughen. We invited him to perform the ceremony because a book he has written has been a great inspiration to us – "Moses and the Venture of Faith".

The stone carries the inscription which begins: "Venturing in faith to build a new church centre…" and which ends with our motto for that year: "With God nothing will be impossible".

May I encourage each one of you to come and take your place within the family of God at St Jo's, and share in the "life in all its fullness" which the Lord Jesus offers. And I invite as many of you as possible to becomes FRIENDS of ST JOSEPH'S and, when everything is completed, to be able to say:

"THIS IS OUR LOCAL CHURCH – WE HELPED TO BUILD IT".
(David Banting: Appeal letter)

The Development Prayer

O Lord God, when you give your servants to endeavour any great matter, grant us to know that it is not the beginning but the continuing of it till it be thoroughly finished that yields you the true glory. So guide us, Lord, in all our doings with your gracious favour and further us with your continual help, that, in all our works, begun, continued and ended in you, we may bring glory to your holy name and by your mercy attain everlasting life, through him who for the sake of finishing your work, laid down his life for us, our Redeemer, Jesus.

We're In!

The Church was built with amazing speed. Having laid the foundation stone at the end of October, 1988, the new building was ready to use by Christmas 1989. The first service was held on Christmas Eve.

This is the first main gathering for worship and thanksgiving in this new church of St Joseph – God's gift to us and our gift to Him. In the Lord you are welcome – welcome to this new church, welcome to the Lord's table and to His grace, welcome into His fellowship.
(Christmas Service Sheet 1989)

The new church was finished by the end of December 1989, so at the midnight service, half-way through, we walked out of the old church and into the new church. (There wasn't a connecting door in those days.) What a beautiful sight and so memorable. We could celebrate Christ's birth and our new life in a new church. God is so good.

Although the connecting door had been planned and built into the wall, it was a few years before it was installed – all to do with building regulations!

Once the church had been built, the old church was reordered and the kitchen moved so that it was useful to both the hall and the back rooms, with a hatch to serve both sides.
(De Parrott)

Welcome

Welcome to the new St Joseph's Church. Come and see – come let us adore him!

Yes, we were able to move into the new church at that most special of times – Christmas Eve. A quiet beginning with Holy Communion at 8.00am, then the Children's Christmas Pageant at 10.30am – unashamedly a party to celebrate Jesus' birthday, and the day ending with the moving celebration and mystery of Midnight Communion. Eyes uplifted at once to the majestic ceiling and simple St Joseph's cross, hearts and voices lifted to the Lord of the Cross, the Lord of the Church.
(St Joseph's Newsletter   January 1990)

The New St Joseph's built, dedicated, interpreted

GOD COMES TO US

"Any tourist will know that England is full of medieval churches and cathedrals arranged inside just like the ancient tabernacle or Temple in the Old Testament." So comments a recent commentary on the letter to the Hebrews in the New Testament.

It continues: There is the chancel, the most holy part, divided off by a screen from the nave, the less holy part (just as the most holy part of the Temple was divided off from the holy place by the veil). The effect, if not the intention, on the minds of generations of worshippers was nothing short of disastrous. Instead of reminding them (as the Letter to the Hebrews constantly does) that every believer has freedom, here now, on earth, to enter the most holy place, i.e. the immediate presence of God, by the blood of Jesus (Hebrews 10:19-22), it taught believers to "stand far off", as if unfit to come too near into the most holy part of the church building on earth, let alone into the presence of God in heaven. The best one could do was hope. Thank God that in recent times things have been changing...."

It is a church building like the new St Joseph's where we can see such changes put into effect. But perhaps they need explaining as to how they are more biblical.

The Christian life and faith are all about switching from putting self first to putting God truly as supreme. The chief function of any church building is to speak about God. I am talking obviously about God as perceived by Christians, as revealed in Jesus Christ and in the Scriptures. God's nature there revealed presents architects with a towering challenge. God is invisible Spirit, while architects work with visible materials. And God is essentially dynamic, while the building, physically at any rate, is inert. These two considerations are daunting.

Now the fundamental insight of Christianity (which has escaped most other religions) and the very heart of the Christian gospel, is that in Christ, God comes to us. That is what the Incarnation and Redemption are all about.

God's coming to us is more significant than our going to him. The controlling movement of the Christin faith is from God to us, and not from us to God. This fits in well with the western "work ethic" (good, even hard work gets you places), which concentrates our efforts, but is profoundly misleading and false to the gospel. The good news of Jesus is that God has freely and fully come to find us where we are, even in our sins, even without all our aid or effort, even when we are not looking for him. Such is the wonder of the grace of God that comes to us in Jesus,

It is essential for the main thrust of any church building to be unmistakably from God to us. It must be readily seen and interpreted as the house of the incarnate God, the God who comes to us at Bethlehem and at Calvary. This needs to be made doubly clear because it runs counter to the habit of mind of many congregations (e.g. "going up to the Communion rail to make my Communion").

I imagine that it will already be clear that the new St Joseph's has been designed and built to reflect this clearer and better grasp of theology. The building is "in the round", actually it is square, which has the effect of bringing the whole sanctuary area nearer to us (with the Cross, and Table and Lectern/Pulpit, which speak of God's acts and words towards us). Indeed, the dais is moveable and can be moved further forward and deeper into the congregation, emphasising even more God's coming among us. The square shape of the building invites and requires the congregation to gather around in response to the Lord's coming and giving, and in the process begin to see and acknowledge others in the fellowship of God's people.

Ephesians 2:13-16:
But now in Christ Jesus you who once were far away have been brought near by the blood of Christ. For he himself is our peace, who has made the two groups one and has destroyed the barrier, the dividing wall of hostility, by setting aside in his flesh the law with its commands and regulations. His purpose was to create in himself one new humanity out of the two, thus making peace, and in one body to reconcile both of them to God through the cross, by which he put to death their hostility.

Jesus has opened up free and full access to God's presence (Romans 5:2) and has abolished all human barriers and divisions between men. We are Christians, and have built a Christian church, truer, we trust, to the gospel and theology of the Bible. The link with God must be open, and the way to relationships with others present must also be open.

Many people sense that our new church is a beautiful and uplifting building. Even though a "modern" church, it has features of design and furnishings and an atmosphere which can still lead to stillness and reverence. At the same time, its lay-out and flexibility can enable more overt expressions of our praise and joy, and a fuller participation. We are fortunate to enjoy such a design. It does indeed speak to us of our gracious God, the God who comes to us, the God and Father of our Lord Jesus Christ.
(David Banting, March 1990)

Furnishings and Fixtures

In the new church, we have some wonderful new furnishings and fittings:

The organ is a pipe-less, computing organ from Makin's, with two speakers high up in the roof. Its purchase has been made possible by a donation from Tarmac.

The cross is a replica (on a larger scale) of that given in memory of Normas Thomas and designed by Brian Templar, in the old church, as is the cross in stainless steel on the fleche high above the roof of the church. The original will greet you in the new entrance lobby.

The table for Communion has been designed by our architect, George Sidebottom of Twentyman Percy and Partners, and constructed by Brian Templar.

The bell comes from Newchapel and is dated 1862. It is operated electrically and will toll before services.

The baptistry is complete, but concealed beneath the floor, directly under the central light, ready to be used after due discussion and when an appropriate request is made. The present font (in memory of Alice Best) has been transferred into the new church.

The wall hangings, the coloured glass windows and the kneelers will only be seen, and then in all their glory, at the official opening on April 7th.
(David Banting: Development Project Update, December 1989)

The Wall Hangings

The design for the new church building included spaces on the front wall for two hangings the dimensions being determined by the architect. A competition was launched to the congregation to design the hangings. If I remember correctly, there were very few entries and the minister at the time, David Banting, commissioned a design from a professional artist he knew. When the design was given to us we decided to create them using a technique called "applique".

The wooden frames were made by Bob Ling and a base layer of cotton calico was stretched over them. Gill Ling was the leader of the team and she brought in Pam Baker, a textile artist based at Old Hall Street Adult College, to give us training and expert help on this huge project.

The first job was to gather fabric in all the colours used by the artist. With Pam's help we set about dyeing yards of polycotton fabric in dozens of colours. We sprayed and dipped the fabric using silk dye so that the finished pictures wouldn't look "flat". We needed plenty of fabric of the right shade, it would be a disaster to run out of a colour before it was finished. Our dyes had to be mixed and we would never be able to get that colour again! Gill did an amazing job in getting thread to match our fabric.

The artist painted a full size version which was traced on to the calico and used as a pattern for cutting the jig-saw type pieces. The pieces were cut and stitched on to the calico with tiny stitches. We worked in the Creche room and what is now the youth Room one morning a week. Some of us had toddlers with us who played with toys whilst we worked. When the new church was built, the builders moved in to reorder the existing rooms, so we had to move into the newly finished lobby.

Anne Causer and Joan Kirkland were members of the Embroiders Guild and did all the clever stitching for faces and thorny bushes. Pam Lord was quite ill at the time with ME so unfortunately she didn't get to the church very often. We sent her some of the smallest and most fiddly pieces to do at home – she had the patience to work them beautifully.

The coloured pieces were stitched on to the calico backing on the frame. It was painstaking work. Some pieces were very difficult to sew as they were in the centre of the frame and hard to reach. I remember sitting on the floor under the frame to send the needle up as someone else stitched on top.

We had a long discussion on how the hangings should be framed – did they need a wooden frame? A metal frame? Who would be able to make it? Would it make the hangings too heavy? In the end we settled on a fabric edging of the dominant blue of the church interior and the hangings.

I can't remember how long it took us to finish but we got it done before the ceremony on 7th April. We sat back with a cup of tea when the last piece was stitched into place. Suddenly, I think it was Olive Clifford, shouted. Robin Ling was "helping" with a big pair of scissors. He had cut the blue edge of the Resurrection hanging. His mum hastily mended it so that no one would ever know. Only those of us who made the hangings know it is there but I confess that my eye is inexplicably drawn to it every time I am in church.

Before the builders hung the hangings on the wall each of us embroidered our names on the back for future generations. According to the Express & Star who ran an article about us, we spent 200 hours dyeing fabric, 400 hours cutting, 1,000 hours sewing and the banners cost £400.
(Val Plant)

A Letter to TARMAC

Dear Mr Smith,

During 1989, Tarmac PLC were most generous in making a donation of £12,000 towards a new organ for the new church of St Joseph's, here in Merry Hill. The occasion of such a gift was not only the building of the new church, but in recognition of services both to Tarmac as Transport Manager and to St Joseph's as organist, of Mr Brian Jones. Sadly, as you will know, Bryan is seriously ill, but we are delighted for his sake that he has been able to see and indeed briefly sit at the new organ in place.

I propose the wording of a small plaque on the organ:

'This Makin organ was generously donated to St Joseph's Church by Tarmac PLC, is acknowledgement of services rendered by Bryan Jones to Tarmac (1970-86) as National Transport Manager, and to St Joseph's (1964–90) as Organist and Choirmaster."

Thank you again for Tarmac's generosity.

Yours sincerely,

David Banting.

And so, after the long years of planning and anticipation, of building and fund raising, and not forgetting that Albert wore his wife's swimming costume, the day of dedication for the church of St Joseph of Arimathea arrived.

Dedication of the new District Church of St Joseph of "Arimathea 2.30pm Saturday April 7th, 1990.

Members of the District Church Committee of St Joseph's stand and say:

The people of St Joseph's, under the leadership of their former District Minister, David Banting, after much prayer and discussion took a decision of faith to build a new Church to the glory of God with the unanimous support of the Vicar and Parochial Church Council.

In order to provide additional facilities for the Church family of St Joseph's and for the community of Merry Hill, they also decided to refurbish the existing buildings to create a new Church Centre, to enable it to be better equipped for that service.
Now that work has been completed and we stand in it and are glad.

Representative of the Builders – The Site Foreman
Bishop, we ask you to accept this new Church and Church Centre. It is the work of our hands, the product of our skill. May it fulfil the purpose for which it has been built, to be used in the service of God by the people of this parish.
(He hands the keys to the Bishop.)

Architect – George Sidebottom
Bishop, we have designed this Church, in collaboration with the people of this Church, to the glory of God. We believe it to be well and truly built. We ask you to accept this building from our hands.
(He hands the plans to the Bishop.)

Vicar
Bishop, on behalf of the people of this parish, I ask you to dedicate this Church and Centre to the Glory of God.

Building Committee Chairman
Bishop, as the old Church was dedicated to St Joseph of Arimathea, a follower of Jesus in faithful and courageous devotion, so we would like this new Church dedicated to him.

Bishop
We thank each one of you for the work and vision offered to God this day. We will gladly dedicate this Church and Centre.

Vicar
We will join together in saying a prayer from the dedication service of the original building in 1955, as a reminder of our link with the past and the continuity of the work.

People
O eternal God, mighty in power and of majesty incomprehensible, whom the heaven of heavens cannot contain, much less the walls of temples made with hands, who hast been graciously pleased to promise Thy special presence where two or three are gathered together in Thy name: Vouchsafe, O Lord, to be present with us whio are gathered here to set apart this place to the honour of Thy great name. Accept, we beseech Thee, at our hands this house for the promotion of Thy glory, the ministry of Thy Word and sacraments, and the salvation of all people – through Jesus Christ our Lord and Saviour. Amen.

Bishop
Brothers and Sisters in Christ, we have met today as the family of God, in our Father's presence, to dedicate this

building for the worship of Almighty God, and for the strengthening of His Kingdom in this area.

The heaven of heavens cannot contain God, how much less should we support that He lives in this or that building.

Your Word reminds us that you seek to dwell in the hearts of your people to make them a royal priesthood, a dwelling place for your glory.

We rejoice at the completion of this house of prayer and service, where God's truth will be made known, and His people strengthened in their faith and equipped for service in the world. With praise and thanksgiving, we dedicate these buildings to the glory of God and offer them to Him as a place set apart for His glory.

People
Amen.

Bishop
By virtue of our office as Bishop, I now declare this house to be dedicated for the worship and glory of Almighty God, Father, Son and Holy Spirit. Amen.

From the architect....

Dear David,

Thank you for your very kind letter which was waiting for me when we restarted work after Easter. I do very much appreciate your taking the trouble for something which has been a large part of both our lives for the last four years.

I am both pleased and as you say, proud, on behalf of both John and myself that people genuinely seemed to take to the church so readily and to find it a welcoming and uplifting building. The original vision that we had for the building was carried through very faithfully into the executed work and it is not often that that happens!

The conversion of the old buildings did, I think, surprise many people who did not quite realise what we were trying to achieve there. I do hope that it will enable your people there to take on board the expansion of their work in the community.

I have rarely received such a measure of cooperation and understanding as I did from you and the Building Committee and the fact that this was sustained throughout the entire process is even more unusual. There must be stages in all such projects when people feel "it will never happen", but under God, it did. I do agree with you that your people were splendid throughout – even the criticism was constructive, and I never mind that.

I do wish for you and your family every happiness in your new living. I am sorry that we did not have much time to talk on April 7th, but we shall, I hope, meet again in the not too distant future.

Thank you again for all your help and interest.

George Sidebottom. *(Architect of St Joseph's Church)*

The last word on building

The building of a new church began with a vision, given to Gordon Rostance, so it is fitting that he should have the last word on this subject.

Have you ever stopped to think how privileged we at St Joseph's have been? Yes – privileged! We were given the very real privilege of helping to build this splendid new church – a church that will be here long after we have gone – a church to which ministers, wardens, organists, choristers, mums and dads and boys and girls of the future – whom we shall never know – will come here to worship God, to be baptised and then confirmed, to marry and to take leave of their loved ones – all in this church we helped to build.

How many people of our day and generation have been given such a privilege? How many people can say – as we can say – this is the church we helped to build – not only for ourselves, but for all the people of our district?

And have you ever thought of bringing your family and friends from far and wide to see our new church? We should be keen to do so, for are we not God's chosen people – chosen to build a new church in His name and to His Glory – here in Merry Hill.

And now, can you remember what it was like here at St Jo's just two years ago – before we had the new church and the splendid church centre next door? Or, if you didn't come to St Jo's in those days, can you imagine what it was like?

Perhaps I should remind you. There was the much smaller church itself, built in the 1950s as a 'chall', so it had to double up as a church hall whenever required, for all major activities and occasions, such as Harvest Supper and the Christmas Party. And do you remember those hard, wooden chairs?

Then, behind the church, there was the "Back Room", used for all meetings of any size, plus the Play Group as now on two mornings a week, as well as the Guides and Brownies – not to mention the Summer and Autumn Fairs or the Harvest Supper and Auction, and the Christmas Party.

There were also two much smaller rooms – not nearly so presentable as they are now -plus a hopelessly inadequate kitchen with an antiquated gas cooker, and woefully sub-standard toilets. And most of all, a chronic lack of space for the storage of anything that needed to be out of sight when not required – crockery, toys, motor mower and garden tools, Bibles, Prayer Books, hymn books, spare chairs – everything!

So, you can well understand the anxiety with which a few of us, with David our then minister, started to talk and think about a possible re-ordering or even a possible extension. We went on, with much discussion, much time spent in prayer – both personal and corporate – and also in preliminary consultation with the architect. And you will also understand the anxiety and trepidation with which, one morning in the summer of 1985, as I lay in bed, just between sleeping and waking, I heard a very loud, deep and very clear voice say, "Build My Church". When I told David about this, he said, "Well, the Lord does sometimes speak to people in that way, and in fact you are in very good company, because in exactly the same words, God once told St Francis of Assisi to build a church."

Much encouraged, we went ahead with our discussions of all the various options and possibilities. The DCC appointed a Buildings' Committee which eventually authorised the Architect to prepare preliminary plans and estimates for a proposed extension of the church on the side away from the road. This was decided on after much trying out by the two wardens, Norman Walthew and John Higgs, of different experimental layouts to turn the whole church to face in a completely different direction.

We also organised a half-night of prayer and told the 1987 Church Annual Meeting about the proposals. That meeting accepted as the Lord's will that St Joseph's should grow – both spiritually and physically – and we were authorised by the church membership to continue with our planning.

There had been plenty of consultations with the diocesan authorities at Lichfield, so now we were able to submit full details and estimates to a meeting held here at St Jo's in June 1987 of the Diocesan Advisory Committee, which advises the diocese on all matters and proposals affecting church buildings. To our great surprise and encouragement, the Advisory Committee not only agreed that St Jo's ought to be extended, but also encouraged us to go ahead with the much larger and more expensive proposal for building a new church.

By then, David our Minister had made his own vital contribution, and we believe he was led by the Lord to do so. He obtained for each member of the Building Committee a copy of the book "Moses and the Venture of Faith", by Michael Baughen. This title was chosen by Michael Baughen to express what he called the Moses Principle – a principle which he himself had first adopted in the 1960s when he had been responsible for two large congregations, first one in London and then the other in Manchester. By that principle, he inspired each of those two congregations to carry through to a triumphant conclusion - by direct giving alone – a large-scale building project very similar to our own.

The Moses Principle is based simply on Moses' faith in a great God, and that same principle has carried us forward, we believe, in all the marvellous progress we've been able to make over these last six years – progress that has included so many wonderful things. I have time now to mention just two:

Our placing of the order with the building contractors in October 1988 was followed by one of the mildest winters on record.

The unstinting generosity of so many people and organisations – not least Tarmac Plc who so very kindly agreed to meet the entire cost of our fine new electronic organ, as a tribute to our former organist and choir master (the late Mr Brian Jones) who was for many years the Company's Transport Manager.

And we still believe the Moses Principle – our faith in a great God – will see us through, but it is very necessary we should keep on enquiring of the Lord how it shall be done.

And it is also essential we should still persevere with all our efforts – whether as I individuals or as a church – to ensure that, with God's help, we really can clear the whole project of debt, and in the shortest possible time.
(Gordon Rostance, November 1991)

Chapter 5
Onwards and Upwards

The completion of the new church must have generated a huge sigh of relief. All was accomplished. But, of course, the building was completed in order to be used. This was not an end, but a beginning. A new chapter of ministry was about to begin. New church; new minister; what would the 1990s bring?

Just a few of my memories

The Revd Michael Hunter arrived at St Joseph's at the same time as the new building. He offers some highlights from his ministry at St Joseph's:

- Sitting on comfortable chairs with the marvellous wall hangings and beautifully shaped roof.
- The sense of fellowship and community among the variety of church members and the mix of spiritual and social activities.

- Why St Jo's? Sir Charles Marston, who gave the land, was into the Glastonbury legend and specifically asked that this be the dedication = the only C of E church so dedicated in England. (Of course, it also attracted a number of phone calls along the lines of: *'Father, what time is Mass?!'*)
- The way that the Christian Response Mission (sounds an archaic term now!) helped the discovery, use and development of the gifts of so many church members. How this then spilled over into developing a more effective but relaxed pastoral care network.
- The Home Groups, people's eagerness to grow and how this happened for different of them in different ways.
- A solid core - deeply rooted and well taught, who looked to God to continue to build His church and were eager for growth.
- Not always getting it right but the willingness to get up and give it another go.
- Knowing that many people were praying – and having one person who prayed each week for some of my diary items – thank you, Joan.
- Moving out of 100 Bellencroft in July with the builders' assurance that the extension work would be far enough completed for us to move back in by the start of the September term! Eventually moving back in just before Christmas – thank you, Olive Lowndes, for making your house over to us and moving in with your sister for all those months! That speaks volumes about St Jo's.
- Discovering that a Flower Festival could be such a powerful way in which to tell the story of Jesus

(both to church members and to those we would never normally have seen.)

- The sacrifices made to pay for the new building. The midnight service on Christmas Eve when, to add to all the magic of that night and the candlelight service, we were able to announce that the Diocesan loan that had made possible the building had been fully repaid – EARLY!
- The Servant King as a central theme
- The emotion in the Sunday services after the Dunblane massacre and then again after Horrett Campbell's attack at St Luke's School
- Negotiating the sometimes-tricky relationships with the other Penn Fields churches, especially with the 'grown up daughter church' being stronger than the mother!
- The Bishop's Certificate groups and the growth of lay ministry of various kinds and the fellowship among those who took up leadership positions
- The good mix of age and the way that our girls found it (and Wolverhampton) such a good home – even if they sometimes thought that we were painfully slow to move forward!
- In the years since we left, hearing – and occasionally seeing – how the life and fellowship of St Jo's has continued to grow and develop.

(The Revd. Michael Hunter)

O Christmas Tree.... (or should that be Chrismon Tree?)

We have had a Chrismon Tree in church at Christmas since 1990-91, and it serves as a witness to God's love and goodness to us as we thankfully use our new church. The idea came from a friend at Beckminster church, who always have one, but originally from America. The Chrismon Tree which points to heaven is evergreen, symbolising eternal life, which is God's free gift to us all. It provides a background for the white lights which remind us of Christ, who is the light of the world. The white and gold Chrismons, or Christ's Monograms, are Christian symbols used to remind us of the various aspects of our faith and to proclaim the name, life and saving power of Christ.

All the Chrismons were made by St Joseph's church family, young and old, and are either white or gold. White suggests the innocence, purity and perfection of Christ, and gold is the symbolic colour for the glory and majesty of God. At Christmas 1995, the symbolism of the Christmas tree was explained and some of the children put a Chrismon on the tree and explained its significance. (This is perhaps something that we could do again as I am sure a lot of people will have forgotten the meaning, or don't even know.)
(De Parrott)

Opening the Baptistry

On Saturday June 6th (1992), about 50 people from St Joseph's and St Michael' came together for the baptism of Edward, a 9-year-old boy from St Michael's, who wished to be baptised by immersion.

We began with 'Come down O Love Divine' and then had prayers, readings and a homily before the water was blessed and we all joined in the Creed. Edward then renounced his sin, was anointed with oil and then professed his faith. This was done very symbolically; as Edward was asked if he believed in God as Creator and replied, "I do", he went down one step into the water. He went down another step as he answered that he believed in Jesus, God's Son, and another as he confessed his belief in the Holy Spirit. He was now standing in the baptistry ready for Father John to baptise him, which he did by ducking him under the water three times, in the name of the Father, Son and Holy Spirit. As Edward came up the third time, everyone began to clap! After a hymn, while Edward dressed, we all processed up to St Michael's for the celebration of the Eucharist.

The procession was led by the Church Banners and we were accompanied by a policeman! It gave us a chance to meet members of the other church. At St Michael's we celebrated the Eucharist together; we from St Joseph's were not able to receive the elements, but we were all invited to come for a blessing. Father John blessed Michael (Hunter) and Michael was able to bless Father John. We all enjoyed a cup of tea afterwards. Many of us found that we had not been inside one another's church

before and we agreed that we must share things more often!
(Linda Hunter)

From Generation to Generation

As well as being married at church by the Rev Michael Hunter I bought my own children to St. Joe's, again each at a few days old, and their time at St. Joe's mirrored my own going through Sunday school, Pathfinders and Youth Group.
(Liz Evans)

The Flower Festival (September 1992)

With the support of Michael Hunter and the promise of help from the Wall Heath Flower Club, it was decided to host a Flower Festival at St Joseph's in September 1992

In order to finance the festival, there would need to be fund raising, but we had a year to plan social events. Lots of happy memories of these events, supported by St Jo's folk and others.

Skittles with the children in the afternoon, and Roger at the helm. Everything went smoothly and in keeping with St Jo's tradition if wouldn't have been proper without some food. 'Hot Dogs' were the order oif the day for children and Ploughman's supper for adults in the evening. Happy memories of folk enjoying themselves and taking part.

Penn Choral Society entertained us: men in bow ties and flower buttonholes and ladies in long dresses. The singing was superb.

The Scottish evening was extra special, starting Michael suitably attired in kilt and sporran doing the Scottish sword dance with everyone clapping in time to the music.

Finally – opening day of the festival – the Life of Jesus. The lobby had the Sunday School children's display – a garden with a wishing well. Each child made a small flower arrangement all different colours and very pretty, which they placed around the well, so made the garden of flowers.

In the hall was a very attractive display of the kneelers the ladies of St Jo's and others had worked so hard and stitched. Such a colourful display of beautiful work, the theme of blue for the edges and a great variety of coverings – forces badges, flowers, brownies and guides.

Our church was alive with displays of colour and beauty that far exceeded expectation. So many visitors, people coming back a second time to bring relatives and friends, and the kind comments were very heartening. What a weekend it turned out to be! So many happy memories, people talking, smiling, happy.

Monday morning was nearly finished, but not quite. We had arranged to collect anyone from Merry Hill House and Langley Court who wishes to visit. There was Linda Hunter, always willing to help, very slight in stature pushing the largest of wheelchairs imaginable. We were all so helplessly laughing – it looked so funny, before we realised that she needed to be rescued. The residents were delighted and very moved by what they saw.

Happy times with lovely memories; a joy to remember.
(Jean Cholmondeley)

Jubilee 2000

In 2000, we joined in 'Drop the Debt', by holding a vigil outside the church, and in Birmingham. Some of us went to Germany as well. It was non-stop travel on the ferry and through the night to Cologne by coach, and then we took part in a rally there.

Easter 2001, we had the cross shrouded with purple cloth and a crown of thorns during Lent, then Easter Day covered in daffodils and flowers – a true picture of the glory of Easter.

Quiet weekends away at Quinton and Shallowford, where there was fellowship, learning, laughter and fun to be had by all.
(De Parrott)

Play group Memories   Nativity Play

We had been practicing our Nativity play and came to the dress rehearsal. We had all the costumes but couldn't find the bag of lambs for the shepherds to hold. We looked high and low, no lambs. Never mind, we can do without them. The morning of the of the play the parents were in church waiting for us, the children were excited and all in costume. Suddenly, in comes Auntie Glennis! She has found the bag of lambs in the cupboard under her stairs. The excited children forgot all about what they were supposed to be doing and wanted whatever Glennis had in her big bag.

The play went on but not only did the shepherds have a lamb each, the wise men also wanted to have a lamb to carry. When we tried to swap them for the gold, frankincense and myrrh the boys went tearful and we couldn't have them crying in front of parents, so they carried lambs to the manger too. We came to the part of the story when we sang Away in a Manger, I couldn't see Baby Jesus so I reached over to move Mary's cloak so that the baby could be seen. Shock horror! She wasn't holding Baby Jesus! He was in the hall. It was yet another lamb!
(Val Plant)

Resident Ministers come and go, with regularity. When Michael Hunter moved to pastures new, it was the turn of Phil Cansdale to fill his shoes. The faces change – but the memories go on.

Top Ten Memories of life at St Jo's

1. Food.

I knew from the spread of food at my licensing service in 2003 that we were onto something good. There's something about a community of people who know how to do hospitality and are generous at inviting everyone to take part. Of course, having the "Balti Palace" just over the road from church needed all sorts of pastoral visits over my time there, as well as a great venue for a leaving party in 2009.

2. Children and young people

It was always the commitment to work with children and young people which drew us to St Jo's. When we arrived, Lottie was just about to start primary school, and Hamish was three years old! During our time there, Barney was born, and so all three children really benefitted from being part of a church where they could belong, get involved, grow faith and have fun. I'm so grateful to God – and to all at St Jo's – that they were able to have this foundation in faith and see such a sense of welcome at the heart of a local church.

3. START course

It was very early on in our time in Wolverhampton that CPAS produced a new resource called "START", a six-week introduction to the Christian faith. I ran well over a dozen courses, beginning in Bellencroft Gardens, but also hosting the course at church, in other people's homes, and once or twice in the Merry Hill pub. It just seemed to "fit" where we were at as a church, and time and time again it was such a privilege to see people come to faith over the six evenings of the course. I'm especially grateful for the ways in which we encouraged baptism families to get involved, and from there see them step into Messy Church, getting confirmed, and getting involved.

4. Messy Church

We wouldn't have called it "Messy Church" when we started, but we found ourselves learning a lot about different ways of doing and being church – especially with children and families. The morning congregation were very forgiving and allowed us to be making all sorts of mistakes as well as getting a few things right. Some of this grew into "THE NOISE", a monthly Sunday morning event with two worshipping communities in the building at the same time. It grew into our work with schools too, and for me the privilege of getting involved at both Bhylls Acre and Warstones primaries. And the highlight of the year – and still very much in my memory – were the annual holiday clubs: Shrek; Charlie and Chocolate Factory; Wall-E. The teams involved in those were some of the best teams I have ever been part of, and an amazing mix of creativity, fun, energy and inspiration.

5. Baptisms

A church with a baptistry… that all took a bit of getting used to. I'm not sure it worked for the first couple of years whilst I was at church, and that coincided with no requests. But then we fixed the heating pump... and the requests started coming. What an honour to baptise a number of young people and adults, though I can also remember a health and safety fail when one person fell into the baptistry and did themselves a bad injury!

6. Growing Leaders

We ran a couple of Growing Leaders courses, which saw a couple of dozen of people at least step forward into leadership, "being led more by Jesus, leading more like Jesus, leading more to Jesus." And alongside this the excitement of seeing people grow in faith and serve in a myriad of different ways, in the workplace, in the community, in the local church and further afield. I'd want to pay testimony also to authorised ministers, churchwardens, DCC members, and those who served on the staff team as an amazing group of colleagues to be sharing ministry and mission with.

7. Worship

Sunday morning bands. St Jos's choir, Kids Choir, and various musical evenings. Christmas carol singing in the pub and residential homes. Music was never far behind when St Jo's met together. Installing a new sound system and projection ability always felt a big step to take but helped us hugely. My thanks to everyone for allowing me as resident minister to jump onto the piano from time to time!

8. Community

I can't begin to say how much time at St Jo's taught me about being a local church at the heart of its community. Serving its neighbours, caring for the vulnerable, and with a desire to reach out to people of all ages of life and stages of faith. A vision for discipleship which is everywhere, every day, for everyone and in everything. I recall some big – and tough – funerals, a few weddings, and a lot of baptisms. "Onwards and Upwards", our 50th+ anniversary in 2005.

9. Glennis

Enough said.

10. Love

We had taken about three years choosing the new signs outside, including my name. (There was always a sense of irony that it was installed just before I announced I had a new job.) It is this loving community that we most benefitted from and will always fondly remember. The many kindnesses of neighbours. The support of many friends. The sense of partnership across the parish, and ambitious desire to live for Jesus in Wolverhampton and beyond. And for that – and so much more – we are hugely thankful.

(The Revd Phil Cansdale, Resident Minister, Spring 2003 – Summer 2009)

Onwards and Upwards: St Joseph's celebrates 50 years of life, 2005.

I find it a privilege and pleasure to be part of the team responsible for leading St Joseph's. I hope that, like me, you'll be encouraged and fired up. Together, we can continue "onwards and upwards" pleasing and serving God as we look to future chapters of the life of the church.

Looking back
Sir Charles Marston loaned a site of five acres for a Mission Church to be built in Merry Hill. This would be a church dedicated to St Joseph of Arimathea to serve the growing community that would one day cover the area.

Looking around
And so the venture of faith continues. "Start" and "Grow" courses have helped those enquiring about the Christian faith. "Presence" has sought to be a new monthly service for the parish with a more contemporary feel. "The Noise" has provided a place for children to enjoy worship and learn together 3 or 4 times a year. Firmer links have also been made with the residential homes in the community, and local schools.

Looking ahead
How is God calling us to write the next chapters in the life of the church?

People
Churches begin and end with people, loved and called by God. New people often remark on how 'friendly' and

'welcoming' St Jo's is, and in this we rejoice. As we look ahead we continue to hold the vision before us of a church that reflects the love and grace of God in the way we care for others and build each other up in Christ.

Place
The original vision for St Jo's was that it be a church to serve the community of Merry Hill. As a church, God has placed us in a unique place at the heart of this local community. So, as we look ahead, we continue to ask how we can serve the community of which we are a part. Whether it be through work with families, schools, caring for the elderly or partnering with other local groups, we are called to be salt and light in the community of Merry Hill.

Plant
Buildings and fabric have played an important part in the life of each generation of St Jo's. From wooden church to brick, from 'chall' to the 'new' church, we have responded to God's call to "build my church". In 2005 we continue to hear that challenge, and to invest in the resources we have so that the Church and Church Centre can be welcoming, accessible, and adaptable.

Passion
None of the above are possible without passion. No amount of investing in people, serving the community or renewing the church buildings will lead people to Christ on their own. What God is longing for is that we be passionate people, who are loved by the Father, led by Jesus, and powered by the Spirit. And so when we delight in his love, hear his call, and receive his power, then we can move "onwards and upwards" into the next

fifty years and more of God's work through St Jo's in Merry Hill.

Looking up

Look back at the history of St Jo's and you'll see faithfulness writ large; God's faithfulness to the church, but also generations of people responding faithfully to His call. As we 'set the compass' to the future, how do we ensure this continues?

Look Up....

Worship has to be at the heart of the life of every individual Christian and at the heart of the life of the Christian community gathered together. It is the appropriate expression of the relationship into which we have entered as children of our heavenly Father.

Look in....

We seek to enable St Jo's to develop as a caring community by equipping its members to serve God, deepening their relationship with Him and strengthening our lives with each other.

Look out

At St Jo's we seek to help members of the church to live for Jesus within the Church, the parish, their workplaces, the wider community and the world. The outward relationship means that we live out the gospel in all that we say, all that we do and all that we are, so that no part of this world is free from God's transforming power.

((Phil Cansdale: Onwards and Upwards: St Joseph's Vision Statement, 2005)

Away Trips

2009 Half Term Trip to Dovedale House in the Peak District where we spent an amazing 3 days with our young people, our older youth deciding to go for a dip in the River Dove after negotiating the steppingstones. A great time for getting to know them better, including brilliant fellowship with our young people. On our way home we always stopped off at the 'Heights of Abraham' in Matlock and enjoyed a cable car ride up to the caves.

We aimed to go away at least every other year. Our youth worker, Joe Watts, led the Christian input on our evening sessions on this trip supported by Brenda, Phil, Betty and myself. This included worship, quizzes and loads of Fun!
(Steve Perry)

We had a long weekend to Bewdley with our young people in 2011. The centre is run by Sandwell local authority and is a great wooded venue for a group of young people and leaders with activities supervised by staff including treasure hunts, fire lighting, climbing walls, woodland walks, archery, games room with excellent accommodation and food. We were introduced to this venue by Dave Rowe who is a headmaster in Sandwell and was a regular member of St Jo's congregation.
(Steve Perry)

Fairs and Socials

As I write, it seems funny that this will be my last report, after eight years. I have enjoyed it, but it's time for new blood.

Our quiz night with fish and chips has always been a good get-together, and the June barbecue was great it's good to see our families having fun together. And yes, it did not rain!

We had local comedian Doug Parker entertain us in October. He was so funny and his three-man band who came along with him got us all singing to 60's music.

Our last event of the year was the Christmas church family party and panto. It was so much fun, with lots of church family involved.

Our vision is for everyone to have fun together, bring along friends and neighbours, whilst getting to know each other in the church family.

I would like to thank everyone who has supported me over the years, including the chaps without whom nothing could happen. So, with a lot of prayer, Jenny Green and her team are taking over. So please do support them. My prayers are with them, and thank you, Lord, for being with us over the years.
(Hazel Hughes, Fairs and Social Committee 2012)

St Joseph's According to WhatsApp

History is about so much more than just dates and events. It's about feelings, and experiences, and more than anything, memories. During the lockdown weeks, What's App provided an excellent forum for disseminating information, sharing prayer requests, and reminiscing. Little did the participants know – not only were they sharing history, they were creating history. Happy days! Happy memories!

Dan: Can you remember this, Val? "I'm happy cause your happy, and that's the way it should be, na na na na na.

Val: Oh Yeah! I still sing it with the toddlers when I do Bears and Prayers. Fab song and fits any occasion – we even sing it in the Nativity play.

Did you sing it when you were in Sparklers with me?

Tracey: I was thinking about songs too, the ones we used to sing in the monthly

Pram Services with Alex and Jack. Two little eyes to look to God, and The Wise Man built his house upon the rock.

Can anyone remember any others?

Carolyn: Tracey, these songs take me back to Sunday School.

Dan: Even though I've had brain damage, I can still remember the Auntie Val classics.

Val:	Sorry, my selection of songs seems to have that effect. Did you sing 'Sing a little song of happiness"? We ended it with the Morecombe and Wise dance as we left the front of church.
Dan:	I just about remember it.
Val:	In that case Dan, you have the privilege of being part of all the Auntie Val classics.
Dan:	I like Marmite, Sandwiches and Crisps.
Val:	Wow! You sang that one too. That was for harvest. A hat trick of classics! Did you sing, "I'll just blow a kiss from me'? It was for the finale of the Nativity one year and written specially for Sparklers by Beryl Jones.
Rose:	I remember 'Blow a kiss".
Val:	Yet another fab song – not a dry eye in the house after that one. I still do that one with Bears and Prayers too. Thank you, Beryl.
Carolyn:	John always remembers the 'Dropping, dropping, dropping' song he sang in his Sunday school group as the collection was taken!
Val:	The dropping, dropping money was counted in with the offering from main church, but later we sent it to a school in Africa run by Joan and Bryan Cox.
Glennis	Was it a school in Ghana? The children were horrified that they had so few books and wanted their money to buy some.
Dan:	I used to love it when you got your guitar out.
Val:	Ha! Ha! Ha! It was fun. I was sometimes referred to as Julie Andrews. Dan you may

have moved into the junior group by the time we sent our collection to Africa. I'm sure Aunty Glennis will supply the details. What a memory you have – are you sure you have brain damage???

Dan: I reach up high, I touch the ground, I stomp my feet and I turn around, I've got to woah woah, praise the Lord.

Brenda: I just love all these songs. Brings back so many memories.

Val: Me too, Brenda. Dan, every time you remember another, I find myself singing it. Thank you. Think we might have to cut a CD.

Mary: A CD would be great to give the children.

Dan: I've already promised Mum and Dad a copy of our CD.... Wake up Jesus! But this time Jesus did wake up, aaaaaaaaand the waves calmed down and the thunder stopped, and the boat stayed in one place (someone is gonna have to help me with this bit) and they knew they would be saved.

Pam: Hallelujah, Dan.

Val: We had hours of fun with that one, but you do need the actions to go with it. We aren't walking down memory lane, we are singing and dancing down it.

Sarah: Really enjoying reading all the stories and songs.

Val: Here's one to task the memory..... who remembers the memory verse song from the holiday club we did with Michael Hunter on the 'I am the way, the truth and the life'?

Olive Lowndes' banner that she made with her craft group is still hanging in the church. Here's a clue.... Ooh wooh ah aah, Ting tang walla walla bing bang.

Cath: Answering on Dan's behalf... he said yes, I remember.... 'Whoever believes in me will live forever, live forevermore.

Val: Yeay! Full marks, Dan!

Cath: Dan continues.... The verse goes... in the 15th or 16th verse of chapter 3 in the book of John, God so loved the world that He gave his only Son that whoever believes in him shall live forever, live forever, live forevermore. (He said he's had a bang on the head so can't remember the verse number!!!!)

Brenda: Wow, Dan you are amazing. I could hear the tune, no idea about the rest of the words.

Val: You can tell him that I haven't had a bang on the head lately, but I don't know the verse number either!

Pam: This is wonderful to see how God sows these seeds in our memories. Songs, memory verses....and they grow our spiritual lives.

I can go back many more years and still recall choruses!! All biblically based and memory verses that God's Holy Spirit brings to mind. I'm so grateful to my Sunday School leaders at St Jo's from yesteryear!! Time to start writing my memories. You are all inspiring me.

Loads of love St Jo's.

Hilary:	John 3:16. Loving this dialogue. We were still up at St Aidan's for this part of the history.
Val:	Pam, a memory I have of you is of one of Phil Cansdale's "Noise" events, when you were carried on in an armchair to the story of Phil and the Ethiopian.
Pam:	Indeed Val. I'm on my way upstairs to find the prayer book, new Testament and Bible I received for collecting money for bricks for the now community hall, including the 10 Commandment wall panels.
Val:	Wow! Pam that's great! Did you have names on the bricks then? The Noise was fun and very noisy! Shame it didn't survive the move from morning to afternoon.
Brenda:	Noise was fab. Like you say, Fun and Noisy.
Pam:	We were awarded gifts for collecting brick money for the 'old church building', now the 'centre'.
Clare:	The Noise was great. The kids loved it! Plus, the holiday clubs at the same time were fantastic. One of the reasons we stayed at St Joe's was the great kid's church. Also, personally, I love the music and the band we are so blessed with each week.
Carolyn:	Pam, do you remember the Smartie tubes – collecting pennies in them for a building fund when my Dad ran the Sunday School?
Pam:	Yes, we did that when I led Infants same time as Don did Juniors.

Val:	How wonderful. I love the inscription, "a token of merit for zeal and devotion". You really can't get any better than that. That's treasure.

Dan:	I know it's not Christmas, but ah well: Sleep baby Jesus in your little crib; Mary and Joseph watch over you, Angels above sing Alleluia

And Memories from Carl

Carl Rudd followed Phil into the role of Resident Minister, and offers his own memories of his time at St Joe's.

- I am reminded of the amazing work done by different youth workers some off the wall and even over the wall, others outdoor adventures and experiencing living rough in the garden.

- The holiday clubs that involved the work of so many with crafts, games, bible times, the message each day, creative talents, worship team, team leaders and helpers, the kitchen team. So many different themes over the years.

- Seeing the ministry of Adventurers grow to children as it also grew its leadership.

- The celebrations for 25 years of the 'new church'.

- Weekends at home with time to learn and reflect, camping at New Wine, celebrations as we spent time together eating, maybe we should say feasting as we have been so well catered for.

- The occasional sadness with loved members going to glory, although even then to remember their ministry among us and to Merry Hill is always encouraging.

- The growing strength, built in Focus groups, and the blessings hearing from our mission partners when they were able to visit.

- The strength of faith to never give up, to pull together and press on to see situations flourish again, to support each other whenever difficult times hit.

(The Revd Dr Carl Rudd)

THE LAST WORD ON HISTORY
(Pam Teece Remembers…)

*Not many people have the privilege of being involved in the building of a new church during their lifetime, how much less, then, can anyone claim to have witnessed the building of not just one, but **two** new churches. But as the* *longest continuous serving member of St Joe's, that has been Pam's experience. As a girl, Pam was involved in the building of the new church – the 'chall' – in 1955. And then, in 1988/89 she was busy again – on the Buildings' Committee, and as district warden, during the building of the second 'new church'. She has rightly earned the last word in this history chapter of St Joseph's.*

I'm not the oldest member of St Jo's, but I am the longest serving one!

I began Sunday School in 1949, aged three.

St Jo's was the wooden hut building nearest to the new Boots Chemist. Sunday School was 2.30pm on Sunday afternoons.

During those early years I was taught well by committed teachers. We learned choruses: *Wide, wide as the ocean*; *Turn your eyes upon Jesus*; *Two little eyes to look to God; Do you want a pilot, signal then to Jesus*. We learnt memory verses of scripture, all of which have stayed with me through my life. I know that God the Holy Spirit brings them to mind today as needed.

A new church was built called a "Chall". It was to be a multi-purpose church and a hall. Opened in 1955. Together with other Sunday School children we had green booklets to record monies we collected from family to go towards building the new St Joseph's (now the Church Centre). The children have a plaque with the two 10 Commandments boards now at the back of the

"Centre". Money from the children paid for these. I have three book gifts presented to me for collecting money for the church building. A Prayer Book 1954; An RSV New Testament 1955; An AV Bible 1957.

At the age of 13, I became a member of St Joseph's choir – black robe and skull hats with white cuffs and collar! I was a member for many years – 25 on and off. St Joseph's had a Pathfinder Group which a curate led, and I attended. In 1960, I was confirmed at St Philip's. Confirmation classes were held at St Philip's on a Sunday morning at 10.00am. My friend and I would often race down Coalway Road for Morning Service at St Jo's afterwards at 11am.

1961 saw St Joseph's Youth Group appear. A group of us asked the then wardens at St Joseph's if we could start our own group. They supported us all the way. A Youth Club, on a Saturday night open to the community, then Sunday night after Evening Service, a Youth Fellowship.

Sunday School had good numbers in the early 60s – both infants and juniors. I did training at the age of 16 and began teaching in the Infant department.

Being part of the youth group was fun and everyone was supportive. I experienced that when sadly my father died in 1962, he being 46, and me 16 doing 'O' level re-takes - very much a time of 'Footprints'. Jesus was carrying me. Not that I was aware of the 'Footprints' poem at the time. As I was an only child and my mother was on her own, I didn't go far away to college. Between 1964-67 I trained as a teacher at West Midlands College of Education in

Walsall (now the educational part of the University of Wolverhampton). I kept in very close contact with home and St Jo's – particularly with the youth. I was able to take part in some of the fellowship times and it was during one of these meetings that I prayed out loud! As I look at it in hindsight, for many years I'd had such a good biblical teaching that my commitment to Jesus was gradual, not a Damascus Road one. Yet the night of the Youth Fellowship meeting, again with hindsight speaking, I think I had been a Joseph of Arimathea for some time – hiding my light – shying away from speaking boldly. So this was a growth point.

1967 – 71 saw me teaching in Wolverhampton and back into St Jo's family again in Sunday School and Youth Work. These years saw an enthusiastic youth fellowship across the parish. We even had our own group: 'The Campaigners' and played at a church youth Coffee Bar at St Matthew's Willenhall – 2 guitarists (Peter Deaville and David Lee), then singers (Heather Griffiths, Jane Callow and 'yours truly'). These years saw the beginning of monthly Youth Services and St Jo's. 1662 Evening Prayer took a rest!

1971 saw me move to Sheffield to teach for 4 years. These years saw the season of the 'Festival of Lights' opening up the church to the work and empowering of the Holy Spirit – new songs, song writers blessing God's church. I thank the Lord for my move to Sheffield for that short time. A big growth spurt for me spiritually and an equipping for all He had for me on my return to St Jo's Merry Hill.

Returning to Wolverhampton in 1975 due to my mother's ill-health and guided by the Holy Spirit to return home. Important scripture guided me at this point. Proverbs 3:5-6:

Trust in the Lord with all your heart and lean not on your own understanding; in all your ways submit to him, and he will make your paths straight.

These verses have been recalled by the Holy Spirit in times following this.

I was guided to my new teaching job at St Luke's Junior School where I remained until July '95. Deputy head from 83 – 95. I taught Janine Wright when she was 7! Now she's a Lay Reader at St Phil's. A wonderful encouragement to me to see her growth in Christ over these years.

St Joseph's 1975 onwards saw me take the reins of Infant Sunday School leader from Betty Kent the then Head of Warstones Infant School. These years and before saw thriving Sunday Schools. I took over 50 infants from Betty. We had Sunday School Anniversaries in May. These had happened many years before, even in my childhood.

In 1978, St Joseph's grew up! We became St Joseph's District Church. We had our own Resident Minister, the Revd. Alex Jack, with his wife Peggy. Also, during the years 74 – 78, the Merry Hill estate was built. Glennis and Hazel came on the scene in the late 70s. We visited the new homes, led by Alex Jacks. I remember great Family Services with Alex, loved by adults and children.

We managed our own finances; the church committee became the DCC (District Church Council).

1983 saw a new Resident Minister – the Revd David Banting, and his wife Catherine. Two of their three children were born here during the years 83 – 90. David was a very enthusiastic Minister. This was a time for growth, in more ways than one.

1984: I was invited to be Warden (the first lady warden in the parish!!! Ha Ha!). On my own it seemed at the AGM, and for a few weeks until Brian Templar knocked on my door saying, 'I believe St Jo's needs another Warden.' Praise the Lord!

I stepped down from Sunday School leading and very soon Glennis Potts who had been a teacher before Alex left took on the infant leadership. Also, I sang my heart out in the congregation from then on, not in the choir.

Exciting times with David Banting. He enjoyed being busy, with everyone else being busy too! He was a builder of God's kingdom and set us on to building with bricks too! In 1987 we admitted to a storage problem. De Parrott investigated this. We sought God – did He want us to expand St Jo's; to push the walls out?

We had church weekends at Shallowford House. I believe at one of these we sought God about this even more. Out then Treasurer, Gordon Rostance, had a vision – a word from God. He awoke one morning at 5am hearing a voice 'build my church'. God speaking to Gordon. This was shared, tested and gradually confirmation came that we were to build a building for worship 1988-89. We didn't find at the time, but later, the original plans showed a drawing of the church where we worship now.

So the 1954 plans were meant to be Church Hall and back rooms, plus the place of worship where we are now, and have been for thirty years at the end of 2020. Not enough money in the 1950s, so the "Chall" was built. So "build my church" was fulfilling what God wanted all along. It was a privilege to be a Warden through those years with a Building Committee too.

The raising of money came with giving and fundraising. This busy Resident Minister never missed prayer early morning with the builders. Oh yes! The whole project was inspired by Michael Baughen's book, 'Moses – A Venture of Faith' which all the Home Groups studied, and a sermon series too. Bishop Baughen laid the Foundation Stone in October 1988.

Our first services in the new place of worship were Christmas 1989. It's dedication was in May 1990. Before the next minister arrived, De Parrott took over as Warden in my place, with Brian Templar continuing.

Revd. Michael Hunter with wife and two daughters arrived all the way from Uganda: from missionary work with CMS at Bishop Tucker College, Uganda, to St Jo's, Merry Hill! Michael's ministry was one of consolidation and developing lay ministry. We began a new season: a new place of worship and a new Church Centre.

Personally, I had a difficult few years. My mother's health – she died in 1992. School life saw changes in management and life as Deputy Head was not easy. All this happening 91 – 94. Then, due to ill health, I took early retirement from teaching in 1995. I had wonderful friends to support me; a wonderful church family through these dark times. I thank God for 'Hazel Hughes', 'the Potts family'. Also 1995 saw the return of Alex and Peggy Jack to Merry Hill and to 30 Bellencroft Gardens. They loved St Jo's so much that they retired back here. I had to take things carefully for 12 months, yet Michael Hunter was in touch with Lichfield Diocese, with a new Lay Ministry Training scheme about to begin. So, I began and completed a Lay Ministry training course and was licensed a Reader to Pennfields Parish in January 1999.

Again, thanks to God the Holy Spirit for His guiding me into this, confirming with words of scripture. Jeremiah 29:11-13:

'I know the plans I have for you....' He certainly knew what he was doing. Knew all along, having already given me opportunities to lead, right the way through my journey of faith, which began here at St Jo's. God has got more for me to do for Him in this place. My licensing was the best day of my life. So blessed, so encouraged by a coach load of St Jo's family in Lichfield Cathedral. Thank you, God.

A real privilege to serve in this way as Reader licensed to lead worship and speak for God: the Pam who was like Joseph of Arimathea, hidden, quietly following, unsure she could speak out like her more confident contemporaries in the youthful days! Years in Sheffield saw the beginning of a deepening in faith, a journey with the Holy Spirit my guide, comforter and empowerer. I couldn't stand up and lead or speak without His enabling. So Jan 99 onwards and now beginning my 21st year as a Reader. Thank you, God!

This season of Revd. Michael Hunter, until 2002, saw small groups ministry for seekers, new home groups, and a few commissions in Lay Ministry – De Parrott, Jo Collins, Sue Tilt, and in Carl Rudd's time, Krish Birhah.

After 12 years, Michael moved to Yorkshire and 2003 saw the beginning of Revd. Phil Cansdale with Tracey and their 3 children, the youngest born whilst at St Jo's. Families became a big focus. Music ministry began to be stirred. 'Start' courses followed by 'Grow' (with then use of Emmaus material. New home groups developed. We had encouraging children's groups and Pathfinder parents in church. Children's Church was called "Noise", monthly in the hall on a Sunday morning. The Church Hall beginning to be used more community wide.

Also during this season, 2003 – 2009, the 6.30pm service 'Presence' began jointly with the parish, then became St Jo's own, begun by Phil. Heading towards 2008-9, service times changed. A 9am service replaced 8am HC and the 10.30am service, as now. 6.30pm, we tried a different style each week. Then "Presence" remained the only one. Numbers of people going along evening time dwindled, the same as at St Phil's.

2005 saw my health take a dip, and 2009 my first chemo, so a lot of time was spent at home, yet always in touch with the St Jo's family praying and encouraging me. The second time, 2014-15, staying even more in touch – mobile phone helped!

2010 saw Carl Rudd and Aileen and Lydia arrive. This last period has been a season of growth, in touch with the local community as contacts began to blossom: Place of Welcome; 5 Ways Lunches; the Church Centre being used more and more for community use; the St Jo's Café. Focus groups and a "cell" style music ministry deepened. We are so blessed today. Over the years since 2000, prayer ministry has developed and grown. Carl's ministry of prayer and quiet openness to the Spirit in worship has grown us over these times until now.

I am so thankful for all I've received over the many years at St Jo's. A Bible based ministry, evangelical ministry, a parish that has always encouraged lay ministry. I'm so thankful for the years I've been able to serve God amongst such a family, alongside different Resident Ministers bringing their own gifts to help grow St Jo's in each new season.

Chapter 6
The Company of Saints

What is the church?

Ask that question, and most people's minds will go straight to the building in which we gather week by week. Whilst that may be true, it is not really the complete answer. Although *a* church is a building that is set apart for the worship of God, *the* Church is the community of God's people. The Church is alive and active. The church is people.

Building projects punctuate the timeline – offering the memorable dates in which we place the story of the church, but of course, the true story of any church is its people. It is the people who are the body of Christ and it is in the lives of its members that we see God working His purposes out. People come and go; clergy move on with regularity; the story of the church is constantly evolving and doesn't always fit into the neat categories and time scales that we like to use. But put everything together, and it is in the activities of all members that we discover the story of God at work. This is God's church,

God's people, God's work. Each of us is just a small part of the big picture.

So this chapter is about people – just a few of the people who have played their part in the story of St Joseph's Church. One of the first things that I noticed about St Joseph's (coming here straight from a larger International Church in Bangkok where we seemed to have a different congregation almost every week), was the stability of the membership. Thirty years after the building of the 'new' church, it is remarkable how many of our members who were actually there then, and have a clear memory of that building project, are still here now, and have been a part of everything that has happened over these 30 years.

This chapter is a chapter about people. It doesn't fit into a neat time frame, because generations are constantly overlapping and moving onwards. So, starting in the days of Alex Jack, and coming right up to the present time, let's meet some of the rich tapestry of individuals who have helped to form the community of saints at St Joseph's Church, over the last fifty years.

Beginning with the ministers....

The Missing of Alex

This is a feature that first appeared in St Joe's Newspaper in March 1990. Written by John Higgs, churchwarden, and enthusiastic narrator, it was updated by Jo Collins, who wrote the later sections, and entrusted it to my care just a few weeks after my arrival at St Jo's in 2019.

Once, on the green, at a little spot called Merry Hill, there was a little daughter church called St Joseph's. The people there were very friendly and nice and quite hard-working; and from time to time others would come to join them. But they sensed that something was lacking.....

And God said, 'I know what you need'.

Peace and Calm

And He sent them a man called Alex, a sweet and gentle soul who rode upon a bicycle and, to the untrained eye, might seem to be plucked almost from the box labelled 'stereotypes'.

But Alex was a man of quality. He brought the people peace and calm. He sought to speak and act with integrity and faithfulness, and yet without upsetting left or right. He was indeed a remarkable juggler with a fine sense of balance and was much loved.
His lady wife, the Doctor Peggy, too was admired for her gentle professionalism.

On a sound foundation of love and care, ready for future growth, St. Joseph's grew into a District Church, and settled into its ways and felt a little comfortable.

But then, two-thirds of a decade on, Alex said, "I must go away".

And some said, "What shall we do without Alex?"

But some sensed that something was missing and a few said, "It's time to move on".

And God said, "I know what you need".

Ideas and Vision

And He sent a man called David, a young and vibrant soul, who drove a little car which flew a jaunty little ribbon and, to the untrained eye, might seem to have been plucked almost from the box labelled 'stripling from the groves of academe'.

But David too was a man of quality. He brought the people ideas and visions, stimulating and rewarding activity. He saw the bigger church hiding behind the mask of littleness. He taught exceedingly well in pulpit and back room, and through others in the home. His words, his inspiration and his energy brought gasps of wonder. He was indeed a man of extraordinary drive – some said, a remarkable driver – and was greatly admired.

His slender wife, the mother Catherine, tended the home and little ones with care so that David might be here and everywhere, and sometimes there.

St Joseph's ways were rarely settled for very long. Some of the people were extremely hard-working, but there was a certain busy satisfaction with all that they were doing. And many came to join them, and it grew into a New Church Centre.

But then, two-thirds of a decade on, David said, "I must go away".

And many said, "What shall we do without David?"

But some sensed that something was lacking and said, "We need the rest'. And others said again, "We need an increase of the Spirit".

And God said, "I know what you need."

And He sent a man called....

(John Higgs 1990)

Inspiration and Encouragement

.... Michael, an unassuming scholarly soul who moved quietly round the parish, and to the untrained eye might seem to have been plucked from a box labelled 'Academics'.

But Michael too was a man of quality. He brought the people inspiration and encouragement. His profoundly thoughtful teaching deepened faith brought time to reflect and to hear the 'still small voice of God'. His calm, wise ways steered the whole parish through some very stormy waters.

He was indeed a man of remarkable insight and quiet strength and was greatly loved.

Linda, his energetic, lively wife brought fun and vitality to every aspect of parish life and shared her fund of stories about their ministry in Uganda.

Michael saw the need for shared leadership in a growing church. His gentle, persistent persuasion meant that several members soon found themselves being trained as Lay Ministers and helping to lay the foundations for a much wider Ministry Team.

But then, twelve years on, Michael said, "It's time for a move.'
Many said, 'What shall we do without Michael?'
But some sensed that something was missing and said, 'We need to be more outward looking and ready to share our faith with others.
And God said, 'I know what you need'.

Change and New Ways

And He sent a man named Phil: a young and energetic soul who rushed about the parish in a people carrier and might to the untrained eye to have been plucked from a box labelled 'Movers and Shakers'.

But Phil too was a man of quality. He brought the people a burning vision for shared ministry to take God's love out into new and strange places. He was indeed a man with a remarkable gift for drawing a wide spectrum of people closer to God. His enthusiasm and stamina left some gasping but made church life exciting and rewarding – full of joy and laughter. He was a much-loved leader.

Tracy, his gifted, gracious wife, amazed us al by finding time to care for Phil and the children, whilst also having her own ministry in the church, in the local community and at her school.

Life at St Jo's was full of change and growth. New ideas and new expressions of church became the norm. Many new adults and even more children came to join the throng.

But then, six years on, Phil said, 'I must move to Shrewsbury'.
And many, many said, 'What shall we do without Phil?'
But some sensed that something was missing and said, 'We need time to think and to be sure of God's priorities among so many new ideas.'
And God said, 'I know what you need.'

A Deeper Prayer Base and Wider Community Involvement

And He sent a man named Carl, who rode about the parish on his bicycle, or in the family car and to the untrained eye might seem to have been plucked from a box labelled 'Quiet and Reserved'. (How deceptive! We soon found out that Carl's preferred modes of transport were skis and a motorbike!)

But Carl too was a man of quality. He brought the people his deeply prayerful and compassionate personality. This soon became a rock for anyone with problems and overflowed well outside the church into our local community.

Carl had a great backup team in Aileen and Lydia. Aileen generously used her IT skills to greatly enhance our Sunday Services. They also made sure that skiing holidays were organised to give rest and refreshment when needed!

Carl saw and encouraged opportunities for exploiting St Jo's position right in the centre of Merry Hill. During his time with us the number of activities open to all the community grew. 'A Place of Welcome', 'Monthly Sunday Afternoon Tea', 'Stay and Play', 'Community Days', were added to the many already existing outreach groups. Carl was a welcome visitor in the many schools in our parish.

Prayer began to play a bigger part in the life of St Jo's, and Focus Groups flourished.

But then, eight years on, Carl said, 'I must move to Stafford'.
And many said, 'What shall we do without Carl?'
But some sensed that something was missing and said, 'Perhaps we need to learn more about our faith so that we can find new ways of bringing our church family and our local community closer together.
And God said, 'I know what you need.'

And at a time when we are missing Carl and concerned about the future, it's good to remind ourselves that God is always with us and has plans for us.

During the vacancy for a new minister, we are being given a chance to discover and use new gifts. This is an opportunity we can all share. Let's be faithful in supporting and encouraging each other, helping in any ways we can, so that God's love goes on being proclaimed at St Jo's and in the community.

Let's thank God for the many blessings we have received at St Jo's in the past. It we trust in God, we can face the

future with courage, patience and hope, ready to build on what we have so generously received over many years.
(Jo Collins)

And God said, 'I know what you need.'

And He sent a pink flamingo named Butch….
(Tim Eady)

Betty Kent

Betty Kent joined St Philip's Sunday School at the age of 10 when her family moved to Birches Barn Road. That was when I first met her.

After qualifying as a teacher, she taught at a number of schools in Wolverhampton including Warstones. She finished her working life as Head of Warstone's Infants.

She was a great help to many mothers at Warstones and became very concerned about their spiritual needs, so she started in her own home the Wednesday Circle. When it got too large it was transferred to the Church Hall. It is still a very flourishing group, and many have been led to the Lord through it.

She taught in the Junior Sunday School of St Philip's and helped with the youth club; she was for a number of years secretary for the London City Mission and a member of the Penn Wynn Bible Trust.

After moving to Wychbury Road she joined St Joseph's and there supervised the Infant Sunday School.

Betty was a great reader, and wished others to read Christian books, so she set up the book stall which has been a great blessing to many. She was also a good cook and entertainer, and many will miss her hospitality and cakes. Betty was a kind, loving and understanding person, always ready to listen and give advice and help, always showing the love of the Lord in all her works and ways. Betty will never be forgotten, her memory will live on and I hope and pray that her example will encourage others to follow in the steps of our Lord and Saviour, Jesus Christ.

'Be still and know that I am God' (Psalm 46:10) – Betty's favourite verse.
(Mary Grainger)

Teach them to your children

My first time at St. Joe's, although not my first memory, was 50 years ago, at 6 weeks old, on a Wednesday I think, when I was taken to Pram service. I continued to worship at St. Joe's until 2016 when my family and I moved to Bridgnorth.
(Liz Evans)

My first memories of St. Joe's are of Sunday school with the many dedicated leaders and teachers who taught us.

I just about remember Betty Kent, the Infant Sunday School leader standing at the front of the room, (which is where the cafe is held now) next to a table which was always covered in a green thick tablecloth.

I remember more clearly my Junior Sunday School leader Don Bannister and teachers Kath Taylor and Sue Mansell. Many lovely times were had, and a lot of Bible stories learnt.
(Liz Evans)

Then I progressed onto Pathfinders and eventually Youth Group lead by the Rev. David Banting. Many a great time was had here and some fantastic youth holidays near The Horseshoe Pass as well. I went onto lead Youth Group for several years after that with other ex-members.
(Liz Evans)

My first memories also include services in what is now the church hall. I still remember Alex Jack's family service sermon from when I was around 10 years old, on Jesus, The Fisher of Men. Alex stood at the front of the church with the church blackboard covered in a fishing net and then called each child up to pick a fish from "the sea". Each paper fish had a child's name from church on it and we popped the fish into the net.
(Liz Evans)

Memory Lane

Liz has forwarded to me your email re St Jo's and it has sent me searching my scrapbooks and diaries for references to St Jo's. That has brought back many happy memories of people and events. How many people remember the Missionary Board organised by Diane Davies? When Liz took part in the Reconciliation Walk in 1996 (from Cologne to Istanbul) we had a big map where we plotted her progress (through countries that are very different now). I also remember Linda's Tongues of Fire for Pentecost Sunday - such massive red and orange flames!

Wednesday Circle has many fond memories - thanks to Diane. I remember when we made Christmas decorations, depicting symbols of the Crismon tree - I still have mine (not very good but it comes out every Christmas to go on the tree).

I remember how many of us made kneelers to raise funds for the new church. I had always loved the cover of the Mission Praised book 3 and knew that I wanted to replicate it on my second kneeler - which I dedicated to Liz. (My first kneeler was for Remembrance Sunday and was dedicated to my Dad who fought in WW1.) I must thank Pam Lord who transferred my ideas on to canvas. I was so surprised to see a photo of this second kneeler at the end of Tim's email and it brought a tear to my eye. I remember how amazing they all were - all so different and beautiful. I always thought we should have had a 'kneeler festival' as well as a flower festival.

I would also like to add how sorry I was to hear of the death of Jo Collins - I was in her house group for many years and when I was in hospital waiting for an operation she visited and brought me a prayer card, which I still have and gave to my daughter Sue, two months ago, before she had knee surgery. Jo will be sadly missed.

I also have a memory of a sermon given by - I think - Pam Teece on the Trinity, using a bicycle as an illustration.

So many memories and so much to be grateful for! Thank you for the opportunity to go back down memory lane!
(Yvonne Cox)

Mum had to drag me along

My memories of St Jo's begin with occasional family services as a teenager - particularly at Easter, when Alex Jack was the minister. I have to say I wasn't very keen on church going at that point, and Mum had a job dragging me along! However, at uni in Leeds, I became a Christian, so all that changed. I came back to Mum's after graduating and St Jo's was the obvious church to start attending.

I will always be immensely grateful to David Banting for getting me involved in church life - he roped me into the

helping with the youth group, and I have fond memories of weekends away, Tramp suppers, bible studies on Sunday nights after church, CYFA ventures. They were opportunities to grown in faith and make friendships at a crucial time of transition for me, when it would have been easy to lose my way with God. I moved on to work with Youth With A Mission in Birmingham in late 1988 and since then St Jo's has been an extraordinary well of support for me - beyond anything I could have hoped for - in all that God has called me to since then. Thank you!
(Liz Cox)

Wonderful, happy years

I have been at St Jo's for 42 years – such wonderful, happy, fun years. I came through the headteacher from Warstones, a wonderful Christian Head, Miss Betty Kent. She told me about St Jo's which she attended and ran the large Sunday School on Sunday afternoons, which my two attended. Lisa went to St Jo's playgroup and Lee went to Warstones. A wonderful evangelist was Betty. A lot of children and Mums came to know Jesus through her. She opened up her home once a month to Mums who wanted to study the Bible.

I joined Playgroup to help to lead with Irene who was a Christian, and I also helped to run Mum and Toddlers on Wednesday afternoons. We had a pram service once a month in the church with Revd. Alex Jack. I was also asked if I would have a Mum's house group after we had taken children to school. We studied Abundance of Life.

After Alex and Peggy moved to Dunmow, we had David Banting, who was always on the move, full of ideas with a young family. His wife was Catherine. By then, I had moved into Sunday School to teach the infants. When Pam moved on, I became Sunday School Superintendent. I also arranged the catering. Every month David held the Deanery Meeting at St Jo's with about 16 vicars. I once asked him why we held it here every month. He said because we did a full English breakfast. Other churches only had cereal and toast. He loved his food.

At that time, we only had a tiny kitchen at the back – an uneven floor and old little cooker. Once I was putting out the breakfast, and all the eggs was cooked on a tray. I bent down and all the eggs fell on my back while I was getting the bacon and sausage out. Hazel had to get a spatula and take them off my back, hot, and we put them on the plates, because we had no more. A terrible kitchen!

To build the new church, I had a large reel of paper from the Express and Star and put it round the room, so each time the children bought a brick, I put their name on it. We also did a sponsored pram push down Langley Road and we danced a Conga, David leading us in fancy dress, collecting on the way. Each week we did a collection in Sunday School. I remembered when Dan mentioned singing 'dropping, dropping, hear the pennies fall'. We had a memory verse to learn in a month. Most of the children had got it after a month, and they also brought the brick money each week.

After we finished building the new church, we continued to help the children in Africa for books and uniforms and they sent us pictures of those we sponsored. I helped David run baptism courses and films, then I would visit every year on the child's birthday and encourage them to come along because we had a good big creche. We did a birthday card each year and visited until they were 3 years old. I used to tell them about our Playgroup and Mother and Toddlers and Sunday School. Some of the children came. Also uniformed organisations used to come once a month: Brownies, Guides, Rainbows, Cubs, Scouts. I used to work with the Brownies with their badges work. Lisa ran the Brownies and helped me in Sunday School.

The builders used to say, 'You have got a great vicar'. He went on site every morning to pray with them. The foreman asked if he would marry his daughter, so he came back to marry her. He worked us day and night. I told him I wanted a plaque. He used to turn up sometimes at midnight and push notes through the door, wanting us to do some job.

The it was the calm after the storm. The Rev Michael came along. Michael – a quiet man. I carried on in Sunday School. I did 28 years in total. With Phil Cansdale we did lots of productions. I was once an angel, dressed in Phil's cassock and white top. In fact, when we all went to visit Phil and Tracy, he had the picture of me wearing his robes in the toilet.

We had Flower Festivals every two years, organised by Olive Lowndes. Each group belonging to the church did their own display. Sunday School had theirs in the entrance.

Sunday School had a Christmas party with entertainment every year, and prize giving for attendance. In David's time we used to go to Shallowford House for the weekend with a speaker. We had coach trips twice a year, organised by Norman Walthew the warden. We had two fairs each year. Each home group and organisation dressed their stalls. We had outside service and picnics. *(Glennis Potts)*

Fond Memories

Betty Kent: Soon after my arrival at St Jo's there was a flower festival. I arrived one evening and there she was staring at a flower display completely absorbed. She turned to me and invited me to look at a white flower and the amazing petals. She told me that our God was so amazing that he took such care with even the smallest flower. She helped me to further my understanding of our amazing Creator God. From that point on I was able to look at nature all around me with a different eye and more appreciation.

Linda Hunter: Linda was instrumental in encouraging me to be part of a home group. She set up a group and we called ourselves young wives! We all had small children and we met in an afternoon and finished in time for end of afternoon school. It was a great introduction to the concept of home group and a chance to study the

Bible and have a natter with other young mums. Thank you to the ladies from the congregation who looked after the children while we had time for ourselves!

Peggy Jack: During Phil Cansdale's time we started an evening service which was called Presence. It was café style church with tables laid out in the main church. I really struggled with this aspect although I very much enjoyed the services themselves. I was brought up in a strict church setting where young children were not encouraged in the church itself. Sunday School was on a Sunday afternoon in the church hall and we were not really encouraged to be in church until we were secondary age. This new café style church was so alien to me. On one occasion I sat next to Peggy at one of these services and she gently asked why I was uncomfortable. I explained about the service and how I felt. She very calmly and gently told me that Jesus ate with his disciples in many different places so why not church itself! Peggy helped me to further my understanding and awareness that God is with me always in every situation and that all He wants is for me to accept and rest in Him.

Michael Hunter: My mum, during her last two years of life, was in and out of hospital. Her vicar didn't like hospitals and she wanted communion from someone she knew. Michael Hunter took on that role and regularly visited her taking communion into hospital for her. That was such a blessing and a comfort for both of us.

Jo Collins: Jo was particularly helpful to me during a difficult time in my life. I had just lost my mum and my job in the space of 3 months. Two of my important roles in life as a daughter and a teacher had been taken from me and I was struggling to adjust. Jo spent time with me gently and wisely helping me to understand the importance of my relationship with God as my Father. Knowing that he is there and I may well let Him down but he will never forsake me.

There have been many others who have influenced my faith journey on a regular basis including all of the resident ministers at St Jo's: Alex Jack, David Banting, Michael Hunter, Phil Cansdale, Carl Rudd and now Tim Eady. All so different but all good men who have a heart for God's people. They all had different strengths which, over the years, has helped us to be a tolerant, loving, prayerful and obedient church – thank you all. It was a privilege to walk alongside Joy Dale as she explored her calling and the fun we had with her on the way. To the many people, far too numerous to name, but you know who you are who have listened to me, let me cry, let me laugh and encouraged me at the various stages of my faith. Thank you all and may God bless you all.
(Mal Harris)

St Joe's won more than we lost!

Cricket Matches v St. Phillips played for the Betty Kent Trophy. I think we had it engraved so if found it will reveal the years, but I guess about 2000 to 2005. Matches played annually for 5 or 6 years. We played at WGS initially then at the Old Wulfrunians Ground at Castlecroft, then the last time at Wightwick CC. Much fun was had. Paul Darlington returned the first year and scored plenty but Rev Michael Hunter responded in kind. I can't remember who won each match but St. Joe's definitely won more than we lost. We had cake and a beer afterwards. New faces emerged. Support on the fair-weather evenings was tremendous for both sides. God's Spirit was so present.

One year we had a squash match at WGS against St. Phillip's. I think it was about 6 each side, largely all male but Hilary B played for us. St. Joe's won, just, I seem to remember.

CPAS Falcon Camps bring back so many memories. Coed- Y-Go Outdoor Centre, Oswestry. David the Centre Manager - what love of God he had to share. Chris and Steve Perry, Mark and Viv Skidmore, Mike Bannister, Beryl Zeal, Roger Nicholls, Joe Maggs, Lisa Potts and Cookie Hazel Hughes of course amongst many others. Such laughter amongst the heartache of seeing the need the children had of God's love. Billy Prior and Tony Forza - I wonder what became of them? Canoeing, walking, the foam filled slide, bowling, to the beach, jumping in the waves – some of the children had never been to the seaside. By mid-week struggling to cope, sometimes asking – 'What are we doing here' and God providing. The evening meetings, Mark and Mike doing their Gryff Rhys Jones and Mel Smith chat, Hazel's weather report and score chart, her room filled with balloons, she gave us such laughter - tears streaming down our faces. Songs of praise; memory verses; the children growing to know God as the week progressed; saying goodbye – hard to do.

The inspiring Joy Dale. The bag song and pictures of the bags as they were taken around the world. Supporting the food bank- singing twelve days of Christmas replaced by food items!

Our daughter Emily's baptism in the baptistry by Phil Cansdale. So proud. Singing 'To the River'. Party back at our house afterwards

1992 was the flower festival and celebration of the kneelers. Helen's kneeler 'Jesus - the people walking in darkness have seen a great light.' Still brings a warmth whenever it's on show.
(Peter Hills)

Gaining Confidence

St. Joe's taught me and encouraged me and hence gave me confidence to act on "promptings". This led me to pray with people I met around the barley field and the railway walk and on the canal tow path whilst walking Suki, and with neighbours, including my Hindu friends next door.

We had some very inspiring talks at St Joe's which have had lasting impressions on me and helped me to understand things at a deeper level.
(Val Osbourne)

30 years with St. Joe's - 30 memories

1. Three children baptised 1991, 1994, 1997 and 3 children confirmed.

2. Services at 8.00am, then later 9.00am, one at 10.30am, evening service, one on a Wednesday- something for us all.

3. Rainbows, Beavers, Brownies and Guides for the children. Parade Services with flags and the National Anthem.

4. All Stars, Sparklers, Explorers and Pathfinders, for the children on a Sunday morning. Cell group for the youth in the evening.

5. Wonderful holiday clubs at Easter and in the summer for the children and also for me as a leader and helping in the kitchen.

6. Attending Mums and Toddlers with 3 children on Wednesday afternoons. Getting to know families and making friends. Meeting Father Christmas so many times!

7. Running Mums and Toddlers. Starting termly services in church for the group. Busy, happy, fun times and still meeting Father Christmas every year.

8. Running Playgroup – taking it through 3 Ofsted inspections and also 3 services a year in church. Challenging but wonderful times. So many parties and celebrations - Christmas, Easter, Summer, jubilee, royal wedding, Queen's 90th. So much creativity and fun for all the staff and 25 children. Still meeting Father Christmas! Wonderful times.

9. Weekends away for the children and youth at Dovedale and the Frank Chapman Centre. An opportunity for parents to have a break too. So grateful for these times

10. Time away at Soul Survivor for our teenagers and also New Wine.
11. Wonderful Nativity services when the church was full and the costumes were amazing.
12. Fantastic Christingle services to prepare for Christmas, and the church was full to bursting.
13. Inspiring sermons that were truly memorable at the time, from a collective mix of people.
14. Easter Sunday services outside at sunrise, freezing cold, but exhilarating and followed by bacon butties
15. Baptisms for all ages, using the font and baptistery.
16. Wonderful happy weddings.
17. Sad but meaningful funerals for those we lost.
18. Through Playgroup and Toddlers, acquiring numerous grants that; re-carpeted the coffee lounge, fitted out the toddler and playgroup storage cupboards, bought the comfy blue chairs, the new storage cupboards and numerous toys. Also the new play areas outside, the picnic tables and benches.
19. Helping to set up Joe's café, and welcoming the local community into our church community every week.
20. Helping set up 5 Ways Lunches and seeing up to 40 people attend each month, and this later leading to the start of carpet bowls each week.
21. Welcoming Phil and Tracey, Carl and Aileen and Tim and Julie
22. Saying good-bye to Michael and Linda, Phil and Tracey, Carl and Aileen, - also Joy and Mr. Dale
23. Ordination of Joy, David and Ness at Lichfield.
24. Children taking part in the services, with music, dance, drama, puppets, prayers, readings.
25. Joining in with flower displays at church
26. Serving on the PCC and DCC for 6 years and meeting people from St. Philip's and St. Aidan's.

27. Numerous fundraising and social events. Collecting for Christian Aid, The Havens and The Well. Supporting and meeting Mission partners.
28. The arrival and playing of hand bells in 2019.
29. A church living through Covid-19.
30. Faith, Fellowship, Friendship, Fun, Food, for 30 years!
(Caroline Sanderson)

Loving, caring, nurturing

I cannot remember the exact date I came to St Jo's. I was attending another local church but did not really feel part of it. I wanted my daughter Lizzie to go to their Rainbow group but it wasn't happening so when Rose Brettell said Auntie Betty Chew had places at St Jo's, she joined the group there.

I went with her to her first parade service and was overcome with the welcome and the worship. This was church as I had never known it and I loved it. Lawrie Edge then almost immediately gave me a job and so we stayed. A very loving, caring and certainly nurturing church, I was encouraged and grew in faith.

Bishops certificate, Growing leaders both building blocks, great foundations and a starting point for the amazing journey that would follow that would lead me to recognise God's calling on my life and the journey to ordination surrounded by much loved friends who had equipped, encouraged and supported me for about 25 years.

I smile thinking about the fun things over the years, not being afraid to laugh at ourselves, mischief at Quinta, even the wardens were in trouble; would we win a medal in the rowing; would we win the rugby World Cup while at a day conference; numerous crazy songs for every occasion; bike rides; walks; Mal's face when I got washing up liquid in the dish washer; helping in the cafe, place of welcome, parties, eating vast quantities of cake; fun holiday clubs, enabling me to become Dr Watson!
(Joy Dale)

Elementary, my dear Doctor Rudd

Our memories of St Jo's are Holiday Clubs, we did Holmes and Watson - very imaginative and good fun. Carl and Joy were Holmes and Watson. Everyone enjoyed.

The other was a weekend away at home with George Fisher, and he left us with a verse "Taste and see that the Lord is good" (Psalm 34:8).
(Graham Hartnell)

Chapter 7
St Joseph's Today

The Communion of Saints

St Joseph's Church, 2020. What makes a disciple of Jesus Christ? There are as many answers to this question as there are people who follow Jesus. God's people are a rich tapestry. Here below, just a few of our present-day saints express aspects of their faith in verse and in prose. God is undoubtedly at work in and amongst us.

I Do Have Faith.
Do I have to go to church as well?

Well, not so much go to church…. be the church!

Let's be honest, the church, as an institution, does not always inspire intense feelings of loyalty. Many people say, 'I have my beliefs, I don't need to go to church to prove it'. Whilst many people profess to believe in God, they see little relevance in the institution of the church.

But there is an important fact to remember: as we have already considered - the church is people, not buildings. We are the Body of Christ – the Church – whenever and wherever we meet. The simple fact is, we need each other! Can I be a follower of Jesus Christ if I sit in my house, and never meet anyone else? Well, it may be possible to believe in Jesus Christ if you stay at home, but if I want to be a follower of Jesus, an 'on fire' disciple who loves God and who wants to see God's work accomplished, then it is essential to be a player on the team. Jesus, who's last words on earth were to tell his disciples to go and make disciples, also promises us the gift of the Holy Spirit, in order that we may be filled with the power of God and equipped to live for him.

So what does that mean? Of course, many things, but if we demonstrate God-like characteristics in our lives, then we will draw others into our community. As the people of God, we are called to be:

- A worshipping Community
- A welcoming Community
- A witnessing Community

Let's pray that God will give us grace and strength, to be His people.

Maybe these months of lockdown have helped us to appreciate the value of meeting together.
(Revd. Tim Eady)

A Smile On My Face

St Joe's is one of the churches within my Episcopal Area which puts a smile on my face when I think of it, and a spring in my step when I visit it. If only there were more St Joe's ....

It is a church where faith is real and runs deep, where commitment is sacrificially and joyfully given. It is a community of people hungry to learn more about their faith and to find new ways of sharing it within the wider community of the parish.

It is a fellowship with a genuine family feel, where the spiritual and social needs of young people are taken very seriously but not to the exclusion of those of riper years. The welcome offered to the stranger or seeker is authentically warm.

It is a Church which has a rooted culture of identifying and developing gifts and ministries, where individuals from diverse backgrounds find the confidence to grow and flourish in their discipleship.

St Joe's is not an island unto itself, it is part of the greater whole of Penn Fields parish, and in the long-standing partnership between the three churches there has always been support, enrichment and encouragement.
(Bishop Clive, Area Bishop of Wolverhampton, in St Joseph's Church profile, 2019)

A Welcome

My daughter and I come to the Stay and Play on a Wednesday. St Joseph's to us means fun, friends, and kindness. We have been welcomed since day one and supported with love and care.
(Rebecca Lopez)

Number please?

Are there any human beings out there?
Someone who could maybe help me?
'Cod every time I try to dial a number,
I'm told I have to press another key!

Have robots taken over completely,
or machines that understood one word?
I've spent the morning pressing 'stars and hash tags'
the situation's getting quite absurd.

If I need a speedy answer to a question,
How can a machine reply?
I queue to hear advise that's been recorded,
Then find that two whole hours have passed by.

Finally, I'm running out of patience,
and the end of 'my tether' is in sight.
So the phone's unplugged and safely packed away.
I've picked up my pen write!
(Chris Challoner)

The Facts

(Written after Eddie Askew visited St Joseph's to tell us about his work with the Leprosy Mission)

Tell me more –
I want to hear more,
Told the way I can understand
with humour, with sincerity
      the facts....
Things I didn't know before,
maybe I didn't think before
until it was explained, simply, honestly.
      The facts....

The poverty, the pain,
The dreadful shame,
As the disease progresses
And the lonely days begin
      The facts....

It needn't be like that,
We can reach out
As Jesus did
And touch, and heal.
      It's a fact!
(Chris Challoner)

The Good Shepherd

One day last year on a train journey whilst looking out of the window I saw a shepherd calling his sheep, who were in the opposite corner of the field from him. When they saw him, they did not leisurely walk towards him, no they ran! Oh, how we shall run towards our Shepherd, Jesus, when we see him!
(Delarie Davidson)

A pray I use most days:

Lord your word is full of infinite sweetness!
Let my heart savour every letter;
It has medicine for every wound.
Teach me how not just to learn
but to savour and relish the teaching of your word. Amen
(Graham Hartnell)

Rejoice

Clap, clap, clap, clap your hands!
Be glad… shout
God is about to do a new thing!
Good news I bring: God is about to do a new thing!
So sing unto him.

Sing unto the Lord for He is good,
He is good!

Clap, clap, clap, clap your hands!
His love is everlasting
Enough to go all around…
Enough to keep us all safe and sound!
I'm glad because I was found!
Furthermore, I abound in mercy and grace!

Clap, clap clap, clap your hands!
O what an honour it is to embrace
Such kindness, peace, joy with freedom.
All one place.
I was born in a St Joseph's hospital in Trinidad and
Tobago.
Now I'm gathered together with saints of a loving family
with same logo:
For God, For You, For All.

Clap, clap, clap, clap your hands!
As we do on Sunday mornings to hymns, birthdays,
announcements and in Praise!
Prayers to the leaders, the vicars, the worship band, the
readers!
Prayers to the stewards, the volunteers, the cleaners.

Clap, clap clap, clap your hands!
(Chrystal Taylor)

Born Blind

Reach out and touch my eyes, Lord,
No longer blind I'll be,
Open at last to your love,
To see, as your eyes to see.

Touch me on my lips, Lord
Let faith and truth remain,
That my words may touch others
To set them free again.

My hands, they need your touch, Lord
The sin they'll watch away.
To reach and touch and comfort
Dear ones along the way.

Look into my heart, Lord.
Forgive my sins and pride.
You alone can reach me
My soul in you abides.
(Chris Challoner)

First Impressions

When I first went to St Joseph's Church, I didn't know
what to do and I was a little bit scared, but when I went to
the Sunday School about Jesus, I loved it and I started to
learn more about Jesus. When I learned about Jesus it
was good and I really want to become a Christian. I

believe that Jesus is lovely, and I do believe in Jesus. At first, I didn't have any friends, then people came up to me and asked me to be their friend, and I was happy. I miss going to the church but when this (lockdown) is fully over I will come back and have the best time at church.
(Lexus Silverwood)

My Baptism

When I was baptised and I was in the water, I felt like I was coming close to God, and that I was clean and had a new start in life and could put the bad things that might upset God away. And I felt that the church family was there for me, and I could ask them anything and they wouldn't judge me.
(Olivia Small)

Battle Gear

Your armour? Leave it…. for now
First – go and get up close to the enemy and spy on them.
Now you won't go into the fight blind.
Remember: it's not the people you are about to fight, but the wicked mess that they have become trapped in.

As you put on your armour, check it out!
Any fault could be fatal.

Your boots must be comfy – it may be a long walk to find Peace.

Your belt tight? Good. If it had been loose, so your truth would have been.

Your metal plated vest still fit? Good. Now it will protect you from all enemy missiles.

Your sword just sharp enough to cut away the wrong you found earlier.

Your helmet fit you? Then put it on!

Switch on your radio, now you are in contact with Jesus, back at base camp – 24/7 – even when the fight is at its toughest – He's there.

Great – the fight is won,
Without the loss of a single human life.

What are you doing?
Put that flag down; there's no lap of honour.
Get off the podium, nobody has won a medal.
Just take off your armour, turn around and face those people,
And give them the true friendship they have been looking for....
Good.... Now that's more like it!
(Alan Brettell – in response to a sermon on Ephesians 6)

Black Lives Matter

One of the most significant news stories to break during the months of lockdown concerned the issue: Black Lives

Matter. Our parish clergy produced the following statement in June 2020:

"There is neither Jew nor Gentile, neither slave nor free, nor is there male and female, for you are all one in Christ Jesus." (Galatians 3:28)

Dear Friends,

Recent events in the United States of America have drawn public attention to the systemic racism that continues to cause immense harm across the world. We know these recent events will have caused much distress to many people where past and present experiences of racism have been brought to the forefront of their minds. We stand with the statement produced by the Archbishops by saying our hearts weep for the suffering caused – for those who have lost their lives, those who have experienced persecution, those who live in fear and for those who live with the ongoing trauma that racism has caused.

As members of the body of Christ, we affirm the value and the dignity of all human life. We recognise that every human life is made 'in the image of God', and as God's creation, has inherent value.

As followers of Christ, we have an obligation to work for peace, unity, tolerance and understanding.

As members of the Church, we rejoice that people from all cultures and ethnic groups can worship together under the Fatherhood of our loving heavenly Father.

As people of the Way, we look forward to the time when we will be 'with Christ', when every tear will be wiped away, and there will be an end to sin, suffering and all evil.

We pray for a time where the peace of Christ rules in everyone's hearts and for a time when Black Lives Matter. We pray that God will help us to live together as members of one family at home in the world, sons and daughters of one Father who live in the liberty of the children of God, through Jesus Christ our Lord.

Please be assured of our continued prayers.

Peter, Tim, Treena

Black History Month

St Joseph's member Crystal Taylor wrote the following poem in 2013, during Black History Month. It is printed here as an expression of the unity that we share within the family of God's people, our respect for all human life, and our desire that we may be 'one in Christ Jesus'.

One Love
One Heart
One God

O let's all embrace
The Culture and the Roots of the past and present
Heroes, Inventors, Role Models,
Leaders, Philosophers, Prophetesses and Prophets

O what an honour
To watch and see on live TV
Tributes to those who contribute to the sweet
remembrance

Yes and O Yes, the ones that live on and those here in
Spirit
'Dem gone but never forgotten as time goes by.
It's that time that we can share and wear colours that
represent
It's time that we can sing, dance, shout, laugh, and cry.

To dig deep into our souls
Knowing the roles of others, the way paved
So we can enjoy and express our luxury in Freedom.

So so glad to celebrate Black History Month and bluntly
proud
It has given a clear voice to others can speak aloud
and whether in a group of 3s, 4s, or crowd
the whole idea is to join together as one.
(Crystal Taylor)

Chapter 8
Lockdown

After several weeks of increasing speculation, the inevitable happened. On March 23rd, the Prime Minister addressed the nation and we were put into lockdown. Stay home; stay safe; protect lives. The most unusual period of time that most of us could ever remember had begun. No travel; no visitors; social distancing; no social contact at all. Only food shops and essential supplies open; long queues to get into shops. Shortages of hand gel... and toilet rolls! And then there were face masks; life as we had never known it before....

We are in lock down because of the coronavirus, and everything is on hold: no church, no meetings, no social events.

Easter, the greatest feast of the Christian calendar, when we celebrate Jesus' resurrection, after remembering the agony of Good Friday. The Easter celebration saw the Pope celebrating mass in an almost empty St Peter's and the Archbishop of Canterbury celebrating the Easter Communion in his kitchen.

Thank God that the virus has taught us that Church is not a building but a people, devoted to God and His Son our Saviour Jesus Christ. We celebrated from our own homes with Tim producing services we received on our computers. We realised that we can come together as Christ's people wherever we are, in different circumstances and places. We could view the services on television.
(Brenda Edge)

What is the Church?

St Joseph's Church holds a special place in the hearts and lives of everyone who worships there. It is a greatly loved place, and in this strange season that we are living through, we miss our worship and fellowship. But as we communicate by phone, email, Facebook, maybe it encourages us to think afresh - what does it mean to be 'The Church'?

Of course, the church is people, not buildings. We are the Body of Christ. We are the church whenever and however we meet together, whenever we pray, and whenever we reach out to serve other people. Jesus came amongst us as one who serves. He tells us to do likewise.

So as we pray for everyone who is caught up in this coronavirus epidemic, we are reminded of the importance of prayer, of the importance of being the church, whether we can meet together, or not.

In seeking out prayers to help us through this crisis, I found the following prayer/affirmation on the Church of England website. For me, it expresses who we are, and what we can be doing at this present time:

We are not people of fear: we are people of courage.
We are not people who protect our own safety:
we are people who protect our neighbours' safety.
We are not people of greed: we are people of generosity.
We are your people God, giving and loving,
wherever we are, whatever it costs
for as long as it takes wherever you call us.

Be at peace and remember your identity in Christ!
(Revd Tim Eady – Joe's Prose, April 2020)

Let us pray to God, who alone makes us dwell in safety:
For all who are affected by coronavirus, through illness or isolation or anxiety,
that they may find relief and recovery:
Lord, hear us,
Lord, graciously hear us.

For those who are guiding our nation at this time, and shaping national policies,
that they may make wise decisions:
Lord, hear us,
Lord, graciously hear us.

For doctors, nurses and medical researchers,

that through their skill and insights
many will be restored to health:
Lord, hear us,
Lord, graciously hear us.

For the vulnerable and the fearful,
for the gravely ill and the dying,
that they may know your comfort and peace: Lord, hear
us,
Lord, graciously hear us.

We commend ourselves, and all for whom we pray, to the
mercy and protection of God. Merciful Father,
accept these prayers
for the sake of your Son, our Saviour Jesus Christ.
Amen.
(Prayers from The Church of England)

A Psalm of Question and Hope

Your earth is in turmoil Oh Lord,
The winds and Floods came from the west,
The danger of the virus from the east,
The people of your world are full of pity,
They weep in their solitude.
The evil has closed your buildings,
Your word is taught no more
Where are you Oh Father,
Where are you at our time of despair.

The sun still shines in our gardens,
The light rain brightens the blossoms,
The bees dance with joy
The birds still sing your Hallelujahs.
The sounds of your love surround us
Your servants still spread your good news
Your word for all to hear
At the end, your goodness will endure
The people will be free to dance
The bells of your churches will again ring out
(Andrew Rock)

Covid 19

The clock still tick-tocks, but the world has come to a stop.
It's like someone has pressed a pause button on a Hollywood thriller,
And we are the stars who are fighting against this invisible killer.
But this wasn't created in a studio,
No super star muscle bound hero.
A global pandemic, world leaders in panic,
Economy tumbling and civilisation crumbling.
In isolation we stay;
No where to play;
No family to visit and no friends to see.
Our heroes are head tom toe in PPE.
Keyworkers fighting everyday to return our lives to the normal way.
We will win this battle and this film will roll on,

The short intermission over credits will run.
So keep your heads up, Covid 19 will soon be gone.
Stay home, stay safe, save lives.
(Ollie – Peter Boneham's grandson)

Living in Lockdown

When it was first announced the country would be going into lockdown, my initial reaction was, I live alone and how will I cope? I have been a Christian for many years and know whatever the situation and your circumstances, God will not leave you to cope alone. God's love has been with me constantly through the power of the Holy Spirit. I realised lockdown would be a difficult time for me and I would have les freedom. Not being able to visit my family and friends would leave a big gap in my daily life, be a challenge and more so because I do not have any family in this area. I am not from Wolverhampton and only moved here in 1991 when I took on a new job. Both my daughters no longer live locally, Andrea and family live in London and Marie and family live in Italy. However, I was determined to embrace the current situation and not be swallowed up by the uncertainty and despondency.

My daughter is a Clinical Palliative Nurse at Great Ormond Street Hospital working on the frontline with children who have complicated medical needs. Sadly, several of the children have contracted Coronavirus. I do worry about her well-being and safety and ask God daily to surround her with his love, to give her courage and to protect her. She has seen for herself the heartbreak and hurt this killer virus is doing because two of her work colleagues contracted the virus. Both were admitted to Intensive Care and tragically one colleague died. She was in her early forties and leaves a husband and two children. Her loss was a big shock and affected Andrea deeply and she is still grieving and trying to come to terms with then loss, not just of a work colleague but also a friend. Her other colleague's condition is no longer critical and still in hospital is making good progress. To lose one colleague and for the other to survive is difficult to understand. In such circumstances we have to put our trust in God and pray for the family who are mourning their loved one and that they will know God's love and peace at this time in their personal loss. Andrea has worked at the hospital over 20 years and has experienced many challenges but nothing to compare with this current pandemic.

Prior to my retirement I was a care manager for many years, and so when I listen to the daily news and hear the loss of life due to coronavirus my heart sinks and I feel deeply for the families, staff and residents. The figures are staggering and unprecedented. Working in a care home is like having an extended family and every resident should feel special, respected and loved. When one resident dies in a care home it is near impossible to shield other residents from the things which are happening around them. To have one or more deaths in one establishment is going to stir up so many negative thoughts and emotions for other residents. I have total empathy with staff at this time and I know that when a resident dies there will be tears and sadness, along with the family. In normal times I usually visit friends in four local care homes but now can only keep in touch by phone. I am pleased to say these care homes are clear of the virus. I have nothing but praise and admiration for the amazing job the staff are doing in our care homes. It is gratifying to know key workers in care homes and the community are now seen as important as NHS key workers.

My prayer for the families and staff: Dear Heavenly Father, send down your blessing and heal their broken hearts. In their weakness and frailty, please give them strength tom cope and calm their minds at this time of pain and loss. Thank you, dear Lord. Amen.
(Peter Boneham)

My Lockdown

At the beginning of lockdown, I felt as if my life was imploding. Everything that gave my life structure was being taken away from me. I couldn't go to choir on a Monday, or Wightwick Manor as a guide on Tuesday. No seeing our friends for a drink at the Barleymow, or going to homegroup and no going to church, or entering the church building. The hardest of all was not being able to see my daughter and son-in-law and my granddaughter, Olivia. No more hugs and kisses for now.

It felt unreal, an almost inner mourning for these so normal things. Fear and anxiety had been flung into my life. It was overwhelming. But as a Christian, I knew that I was not on my own, that God was with me in my fear, anxiety and bewilderment.

How do I know this? Because he came to me as I read the Bible avidly every morning. Also, through my prayer time with him, just being still and resting in His presence. It was here He gave me His strength, hope and grace to carry with me as I journeyed on through the day.

I also became aware of the Lord's presence when I was walking in the garden and saw his creation all around me: the trees, the flowers, the bees, the birds and the beautiful butterflies. Also, when my husband and I went out on our daily walks across Penn Common and into the bluebell wood, smelling the pungent sweet fragrance of the bluebells and hearing the incessant bird song that rang around us, I felt the Lord's presence deep within me and began to sing a hymn of praise.

Another of our walks was up Springhill Lane where we would sometimes turn left along a path just before St Anne's Church. As we walked over the field there was a glorious view over the countryside to the hills of Shropshire, a county that is deep within my hearty, and we could see the Titterstone Clee, the Brown Clee and the Wrekin. As I looked at these beautiful hills, I recalled the words of Psalm 121, "I left up my eyes to the hills, where does my help come from? My help comes from the Lord, the Maker of heaven and earth," and I felt the Lord's presence at the very core of my being and His peace, mercy and love filled my heart.

What I have learned in these strange times is the need to come closer to God, to spend more time with Him and to enjoy being in His presence. I recalled the old words:

"Come close to God and He will come close to you."

I personally have found this to be true, especially in difficult times.

When we don't know what to pray, or feel so overwhelmed by a situation, the greatest thing we can do is to come into God's presence and be still and yield ourselves to Him. He is our strength, our rock, our Redeemer.

What I have become aware of is the growing love for one another, especially in our church community at St Joseph's, but also in my local community. I think it began with everyone going outside to clap for a minute for all the NHS workers. It gave us in Lancaster Gardens a new opportunity to talk with one another (socially distancing). Also, this happened again on VE Day when a good number of us took our chairs out and sat on our gardens for an hour or two, enjoying conversations together. Let us hope this continues when lockdown is over!

I have become aware in lockdown that churches may be locked, but the Kingdom of open. It has been so refreshing to see St Jo's exploring new ways of doing church, via Facebook, Whats App and Zoom. Also, I have seen how many of us have kept in touch with our church family via the telephone and the other methods I have spoken about which has helped to connect us together.

Finally, I have found the Prayer Course by Pete Grieg very helpful in renewing and refreshing my prayer life during these difficult times. It has encouraged me to re-commit to as firm time of prayer. To want to make time each day to be with the Lord and to be still in His presence and to learn to listen to what He has to say to me.

Then, Alleluia! Christ is risen. He is risen indeed. Alleluia. *(Sue Tilt)*

The Anniversary

As we experienced Pentecost under Lockdown, Brenda Edge reflected on Whitsun from her childhood.

The Midlands have in the past acknowledged Pentecost as Whitsunday (it was known as this before it became Spring Bank Holiday). It was a big celebration, the children were dressed in white (boys in white shirts), there was a band and a procession with banners declaring that we were from that particular church of Christ. I remember my Mum always had a white dress made for me for the occasion. Not only did we parade through the streets, but the Sunday School children were rehearsed in new songs for them to sing on two Sundays in church. Parents, grandparents and friends were invited to come and listen to the children who were again in white. We knew this was a very special time for the church – we were celebrating the birthday of the church, when the Holy Spirit was given to the Church on the Day of Pentecost. In the Bible we are told how, 'the gift of the Holy Spirit was given to the disciples, people were baptised and thousands were added to 'their number' (Acts 2), and so the church was identified and celebrated in Jerusalem and it met together for prayer and the new supper (sharing bread and wine), and the life of Christ was related to others.

My own daughters, who are in their late 50s and early 60s did all of the above, just as I had done as a child. I just wonder if the same celebration was held in the north. It was a Midlands ritual of the gift of the Spirit to Christ's Church here on earth. I, as I grew, became more aware of the importance of that time, of the giving of life to the Church on earth, the most important occasion that we celebrated, the giving of life (the Holy Spirit) to the Church. A person who believes in Christ becomes a real disciple when that person receives the gift of the Holy Spirit.
(Brenda Edge)

When This Lockdown is Done

When the lockdown's done,
We'll once again clink glasses with old friends,
And talk of plans of future put on hold.
We will walk the wild green hills on sunny days
And visit golden sands with new found joy.

When the lockdown's done,
We'll jump and shout at each and every goal,
And cheer when bails are scattered cross the square.
We will once again be amazed at Shakespeare 's prose,
And dance and sway in clubs to the jingling tunes.

When the lockdown's done,
We will meet new family members born anew,
Talk face to face not muffled through glass walls.
Different generations mingling happily once more,
And reminisce of old times from before.

When the lockdown's done,
We will cross the road to greet not to avoid,
A day at work will no longer seem a chore.
Haircut and newfound styles start to emerge,
And shops will greet us back like long lost friends

When the lockdown's done
We'll kneel before the rail and taste the wine,
Thanking Him that we again can meet,
And remember those no longer by our side,
Thanking God for all the gifts and love they've left.

When the lockdown's done
Will we all go back to how it was before,
And loose the love and fellowship we have found
Or will we still be clapping for those so key,
And ever more be kind to those in need.
(Andrew Rock)

Why?

Why?
God made us stewards of His creation.
We have ignored that responsibility and abused the earth
Rainforests
Air pollution
Ocean pollution
Bacteria has mutated hence coronavirus.

The good news is that
Our God is the infinite
The infinitesimal
He rules over all so this virus is under His rule.

We have turned from God
from love others and care for the needy;
to the God of "me first" and of the greedy.
We have thrown God's laws back into His face – the
Prodigal family.

But good news:
the story of the Prodigal is of our heavenly Father
looking, waiting,
for us to come to our senses.

"My children who were lost are back in my family."
Rejoice.

God is watching for us to turn and take the first faltering
step,
And then He will....

Jesus, I give you my joy, so that your joy will be full.

Jesus; others; yourself.

This is why the Minister leaving his church could say to the cynic who asked, "Where is God in all this?" "You show me where God isn't."

The things that really matter in life are not "things" at all. *(Lawrence Edge)*

I do not know what lies ahead………

The week beginning the 8th of March was just a normal week. We met friends for lunch on Sunday, went for a walk and caught up with the family news. We were both at work. I was out on Tuesday evening. Wednesday, I met up with my gardening group, - gardening, coffee, cake, a catch up on everyone's news and the usual swopping of plants. Later that day I picked up a prescription, went to work for 3 hours for Open Day and then had a meeting in the evening. Thursday was a full day of voluntary work doing school Appeals at the Civic Centre, followed by my weekly painting class and then hand bell ringing at St. Joe's. Friday, I met up with a friend and did some shopping. On Saturday I was team leader for the café at St Joe's, so shopped and was at church all morning. Covid-19 was being talked about, but not in a worrying way. Received a few WhatsApp and text messages, and some emails. On Sunday we met our son and his partner to celebrate his birthday, but things were changing. We went to a National Trust property and sat outside to have our picnic - no indoor seating– it was cold and raining. No hugs, no touching – shared food from a distance, and everyone had hand gel.

A normal week - *life was good, but with a hint that things were changing.*

On Monday 16th I was at work, but it was different, and people were very cautious. On Tuesday I was told I had the choice to work at home the next week – 23rd and 24$^{th.}$ A meal that evening was cancelled. On Wednesday five of us were going to see Military Wives at the Lighthouse. It was cancelled, as was a day of school Appeals on Thursday. On Friday, both a morning meeting and my knit and natter group in the afternoon were cancelled. Café on Saturday, in the church centre was cancelled, as had been both Playgroup sessions in the week. I couldn't believe it – everything was cancelled bar one thing – work!

Didn't go to church on Sunday, as by now I was apprehensive and had decided to stay in. It was Mothering Sunday, flowers came from the children through the post and I spoke with them all.

Not a normal week - *life was very different and not so good.*

On Monday 23rd we were both working from home. A meeting that evening for Café leaders was cancelled, as was The Wolverhampton Skills show I was attending for work on the Tuesday. Gardening group, on Wednesday was cancelled, so too painting on Thursday. A Sunday lunch with the Little Brothers at their new base for the homeless was cancelled and so was a meal with friends. The country was now in lockdown. We carried on, we did our work, albeit from home, did lots in the garden and went for walks. On Thursday we clapped for the NHS and chatted with our neighbours.

Again, not a normal week - *but in a strange way life was quite good.*

The next week things changed. By Tuesday hubby had been furloughed, but still loads to do in the house and garden and we carried on, but life was different. People were at home and the 'phone was ringing far more. I was receiving more emails, texts, and messages from people. I was now in contact with so many people through 8 new WhatsApp groups as well as all the family ones. Streams of messages were coming through and it was a real new positive way of communicating. There was news from friends, work updates, social group updates, church news, family news, funny articles, photographs, jokes, and humorous pictures of how we would all look without a hairdresser. For an hour every morning I was looking at my 'phone! I was looking again later in the day. One week my daily average went up to 5 hours. To think, I used to tell the children off, for being on their phones all day. Again, we clapped for the NHS, and all on the front line

A week with 'new norms'' *– and it was still pretty good.*

Then life changed again, the last week of March. Hubby had the symptoms of Covid-19 and two days later so did I. The next 3 weeks contain very little to tell. The illness was bad, but the tiredness afterwards was unbelievable. Life was based around ordering food, taking delivery of food, dealing with all that did or didn't come and some of the weird substitutes. When has couscous ever been a close relation to pearl barley? Why are there no eggs and no flour? In the big picture none of this really mattered. We got through it, and sadly so many didn't. The whole country and large areas of the world were now totally Covid-19 orientated. There were daily updates and extended news items. The numbers of people in hospital and those sadly losing their lives were now daily statistics. There were local losses and those of people known to us. People I spoke with were scared and frightened, anxious for themselves and others. Faith and God came into many conversations, from people of whom I had not heard talk of either, much before. References made to both the plagues of Egypt and the story of Noah's Ark. Was Covid-19 a punishment people asked? The other comment I heard so often was, "this staying in isn't right, it's so hard, we were born to be social creatures". Challenging and difficult times for so many.

We had 3 children to think about, one abroad, on maternity leave, one in the northeast, working from home and one a paramedic on the frontline. For the first time we could physically do nothing if they needed us, and similarly they could do nothing for us. Skype, Zoom and the 'phone kept us in touch. So, I crocheted a rainbow and hung it on the front door – something I could do.

One of our new WhatsApp groups was in our street and it became a lifeline to many. Everyone checked that all were OK, and at the end of the week we chatted on Zoom. People were shopping for each other, collecting medicines and sourcing house repair and gardening help. We got to know nearly everyone through the group. The appreciation from families was wonderful and the things people were doing for each other, as well as working full time and/or home educating their children was amazing.

We couldn't go out, due to illness followed by self-isolation, but we had time to get up early and listen to the dawn chorus, even to record it and send it to the children. We were feeding the birds more and saw a green woodpecker and numerous other garden birds. We set the night camera and saw the cats, foxes and badgers that visit each night. I watched a Palm Sunday service on television and I listened to Tim's morning prayer – most days. Days at home were so peaceful and we were told the air we were breathing was cleaner.

A **'new normal' way to the week –** *illness/Covid-19 apart, life was still fairly good.*

Self-isolation over, we started to go for local walks again. Posting letters, parcels and birthday cards put a purpose into some walks and dictated the routes we took. Blessed with the lovely weather, we saw peoples' gardens for the first time and had time to admire all the wonderful spring flowers and blossom. We talked with people we met and crossed so many roads to keep us all safe. Highlights of the walks were when we bumped (in a socially distancing way) into people we knew. It happened a few times and was wonderful. We also spoke with strangers. It was so easy we all had the time to stop.

Our energy levels were back to normal now and a lot of time was spent in the garden. Very little housework got done apart from the laundry; food prep. and the odd whip round with the hoover or duster. No one was coming. So was there any point? Easter came and went. Built 3 crosses in the garden and decorated a branch with eggs, chicks and rabbits for the house. Wedding anniversary came and went – flowers came with the online delivery! Hooked on JJ's Christian messages on St. Joe's WhatsApp by now. Looking at my 'phone even more often to get the next one. So good, so much said, and in just one minute – politicians, preachers, parents, - take heed!

The weeks were following 'new norms" - *life was different, but it was good.*

Towards the end of April, hubby was made redundant, as his employers went into Covid-19 related liquidation. It had happened before but this time, it didn't matter so much. We have our home and the children are all working. Sadly this is not the case for others who are, building homes, careers and also educating children. So many people I spoke with were anxious and frightened over future employment. We were ok- plans to build a new garden shed began. I'm hoping for a sort out in the attic–we'll see!

At a similar time to this, the government said that parents, if they wished, had the right to a School Appeal, for their preferred school. So, all the cancelled and any new Appeals now had to be heard. Wolverhampton set up for these to be done remotely, so I was trained to work from home, using Teams, - a very steep learning curve. So now I was working, almost full time. Everything was based around the computer, my i-pad or my phone. So too, was ordering the shopping, buying on-line, and joining numerous Skype, Teams and Zoom meetings. Years ago, we were worried our children spent too long on their computers! We thought they were wasting their lives, sitting in front of screens. Now those same screens are our lifelines. How life changes.

I started knitting clothes and blankets for premature babies at New Cross and also 'paired hearts' for people in care homes, in the evenings with the TV on – even more screen time! We still only saw and spoke to 'real people' in our road and when we went for walks. I told Tim I'd send him some bits for the book he was compiling. (this book – the one you are reading now!) I was under the impression I'd have loads of spare time in lockdown. Still we clapped each week and wondered when and how it would all end.

Well into the 'new norm' now and it's so different - can't believe how busy I am, how content I am - *it's good in so many different ways.*

Life carried on. Our street had a 'socially distanced street party' for VE day and we also had a lovely zoom birthday party to celebrate my sisters 60th on the same day. We sent and received parcels and posted lots of cards over the weeks and awaited the post in eager anticipation of what would arrive each day. We sent and received photos to and from the children and to family and friends as well. As the weeks passed by, we talked slightly less on the 'phone as there was less to say, but I didn't mind. There was still plenty to do. With the exception of neighbours and pedestrians, not seeing people 'for real' was normal now. Family links for us were all remote, but they have been for a long time with our daughter abroad, so in some ways this was a leveller - strange but true.

The weeks are normal now, with the 'new norm' routines - *life is good again*.

Since the ease of lockdown, we've been out once a week for a picnic, sitting by the River Severn. I've delivered a bedding plant to over 40 members of our gardening society, ready for an online photographic competition for the best plant by September. It's Trinity Sunday and to date, I have done 60 school Appeals and have another 60 to go. Still no eating out so I've done loads of baking. A neighbour orders flour in bulk, direct from a mill, another gets sacks of potatoes delivered, we're growing yeast. I've made elderflower cordial for the first time, because a neighbour offered me the flowers, and another neighbour sourced citric acid for me, as it was also in short supply. A bag of knitting has gone to New Cross and care homes. I've completed so many online courses for work. Back in March I did one entitled 'working from home.' I've now just received one entitled, 'returning to work'. Those titles weren't even on the list last year.

I am in regular contact with so many people through, texts, Teams, Zoom, WhatsApp and just occasionally the land line 'phone. Sitting at opposite ends of the drive, we have tea and biscuits with friends. I am now looking at patterns for facemasks. I'm still listening to prayers, hymns and songs on my phone each day.

As I write now, things are changing again. Lockdown is being eased more and more, children are beginning to go back to school, more businesses are back at work, shops are opening, some sport has restarted, and churches are open for individual prayer. Everything is still about social distancing, keeping the rate of infection down, protecting the NHS, saving lives, staying alert. The weather has also changed, so the sewing machine is out for curtains and mask making. Life is still predominantly home based. **The 'new normal' just feels normal now! –** *life is good.*

When we all celebrated Christmas last year, none of us knew what lay ahead. We were hit by devastating floods at the start of the year, which dominated the news each day, and then the news focussed on Brexit deals. The tragedy of the Covid-19 virus was barely on the horizon. We have now completed 12 weeks of lockdown and it is the central topic of the news, locally, nationally and worldwide. The tragic suffering and loss of life is hard to comprehend, and as I write, we are still a long way from returning to the 'normal lives ' we had before. Will we ever? Can we ever? Do we need to?

Throughout it all there were many things I was thankful for: my family, my friends, my faith, my work, my neighbours and especially for modern technology that allowed me to keep in touch with them all. Also, for my hobbies, my home and garden and also the time to learn and enjoy old and new skills and hobbies. Not forgetting, online shopping and supermarket deliveries. Also, for how peaceful live was when there was hardly any traffic. I also managed to watch every episode of Springwatch. There were also things that surprised me. I didn't miss going out as much as I thought I would. I was never once bored. I can happily order food online – I don't need to spend hours choosing it all. I didn't feel any less close to people, because I couldn't be in the same room as them and give them a hug. I also learned new skills, especially technological ones, and realised new things. Worship was fine using my 'phone, via u tube and Facebook, through my i pad or on the television. It often meant I could access it at a time to suit me and also listen again, if I'd day dreamed or missed something. Fellowship is great, as is the joy of worshipping in a church, but God and I are both also happy, when it's just the two of us. I wonder, will this remote, technological delivery be a part of future ministry? Could it/would it reach out to more people?

I have just listened to a wonderful talk this morning that likens us to the disciples. We are ordinary people with an extraordinary mission living in extraordinary times, in the same way the disciples were ordinary people with an extraordinary mission at the time of Pentecost. The disciples were selected and called to follow. They did not apply for the job, were not qualified, but they were to perform mighty acts; to proclaim the good news of the kingdom, cure the sick, cleanse the lepers, raise the dead. Work for which they were not trained.

We were not qualified or equipped to deal with Covid-19, but we were all called to do our bit. We have been separated from loved ones and confined to home, unable to gather as a community, yet we have faced the challenge with extraordinary creativity and determination. From experiences gained from work and home, and using the gifts and talents with which we have been blessed, we can carry out the same mission as those first disciples, to continue to love our neighbours and the communities in which we live and bring the good news of God's love to all.

The disciples through faith and the Holy Spirit did extraordinary things and so can we - ordinary people with an extraordinary task in the 21st century. God is with us throughout these times.

All of this brings to mind, the first verse of my favourite worship song:

"I do not know what lies ahead,
the way I cannot see,
Yet One who stands to be my guide,
He'll show the way to me.
I know who holds the future,
and He'll guide me with His hands,
With God things don't just happen,
everything by Him is planned,
and as I face tomorrow with its' problems large and small,
I'll trust the God of miracles, give to Him my all."

The weeks ahead will no doubt be changing for a long time –*and life will be good!*
(Caroline Sanderson)

Priorities

We are living through unusual times. How can we continue to be the church when we cannot worship together or hold our regular meetings? Strange times indeed!

Yet, maybe there can be some positives to come out of all this. The Psalmist tells us to 'be still and know that I am God.' This is a time to consider priorities. I was really looking forward to the spring – a chance to get out and explore. So far, I have got to know my back garden extremely well! But I have come to appreciate our own parish. Blossom time is beautiful; seeing trees burst into bud; appreciating the open spaces that we have right on our doorstep – no need to drive anywhere else.

And perhaps more importantly – our relationships. I sense a real camaraderie and mutual care and support within the local community. Long may it last!

And underpinning everything, there is an overwhelming sense of God: God with us. As we focus upon the presence of God with us, God in our lives, then we discover a new contentment. To be in the presence of God is the only 'being' that matters. Take time to be still and appreciate what God has put right in front of you – the people who God wants you to support; the small tasks which we feel that God is calling us to.

Make prayer a priority. We have just embarked upon a preaching series about prayer, but prayer needs to be more than teaching – it is something to get involved in. Prayer is the key to engaging with God, and His plans for the world.

Let's make it our prayer that we will come closer to God in this season when so much else has been slowed down.
(Tim Eady – Joe's Prose May 2020)

And so, to Zoom...

At the beginning of March, not many of us had even heard of Zoom. The thought of sitting at home, talking to your computer, whilst sharing in a discussion with faraway friends, was probably something that we associated more with Star Trek and 'beam me up, Scottie', than we ever imagined as part of our daily lives. But five months on, we have all become more IT savvy – we are Facetiming, WhatsApping, Live Broadcasting, online shopping like never before. Even church services have become Zoom experiences....

A Zoomingly good solution

The Lord has certainly been good to us when it comes to technology! Who would have thought that we could all be together as a church by video link? It brings to mind the words of Matthew 18:20: 'For where two or three are gathered together in my name, I am there with them.' So, with more than 30 joining in one of our virtual services, there was a good turnout!

It's been quite a learning experience for us both as we had only briefly touched on Zoom in our workplaces. Jo was more aware of it than me, so we had to learn most of it from scratch. I mean how do you share a recording of a worship song with everyone, how do you spotlight the person that's speaking? What do you do if you accidentally end the whole service by pressing the wrong button? What if the wi-fi connection drops out? What do you do about someone's whose head appears upside down?

We're still asking ourselves those questions! At first it was touch and go but Andy (Wynter) and Tim and Julie were a big help in getting us to try things out. Things run a little more smoothly now, but at first we were quite anxious about it all and prayed that it would be 'alright on the night'. We would find that there was no audio, no one in vision, the Wi-Fi wasn't working, we couldn't share the worship song because it wouldn't play and then there was the time that the Zoom software collapsed altogether. And that was when we had the largest virtual congregation. Fortunately, it appears that so many people were using Zoom for worship that morning that the system simply couldn't cope!

It's great to see that during the pandemic, technology allowed us all be together and see each other again after so long apart. We feel blessed to have it and to know that it's going to be a feature of our worship for some time to come.
(Chris and Jo Strange)

The Zoom That Went Wrong....

The Liturgy for the Seventeenth Day of May, 2020.

Sunday 17th May must surely be recorded as the most unusual service ever to come out of St Joseph's Church. This was the day of 'worship overload'. Across the country, Zoom couldn't cope with the sheer volume of churches who were logging on. Here at St Joseph's, the service may have been on Zoom, but the liturgy that accompanied it was undoubtedly on WhatsApp! We take up the narrative just before 10.30am.

Andy Wynter	Zoom meeting will start shortly
Jo Strange:	Sorry we're having a few issues, please bear with us.
Emma Oldham	The joy of technology. Don't worry.
Krish Birhah	While we are in the waiting room, we pray for Jo and Chris as they overcome the technical problems. You've got this, guys.
Rose Brettell	Using Andy's link at the moment.
Crystal Taylor	In Jesus name, free up the airwaves.
Emma Oldham	I've been taken out. Says link not available.
Chris Perry	Yes, and us. Joining again.
Chris Strange.	We're going to send a new link shortly as the other one isn't working, so please hang on.

Emma Oldham	It says meeting ID is not valid.
Mary Peters	Yes, that's fine. Love to you all.
Andy Wynters	Use new link above to join.
Chris Perry	In!!!
Krish Birhah	We are in too. Yippie!
Cath Fox	We aren't!!
Rose Brettell	In, but not seeing Tim. Just the outside of the building.
Cath Fox	Got it. We are in!
Emma Oldham	Can everyone mute their audio pls. If you touch your screen it should mute.
Justin Scriven	This link would not allow us to access through phone. Couldn't open through laptop.
Emma Oldham	If you just go into the Zoom app, you can access from anywhere. Just type the numbers in as meeting id. I'm using my tablet without the link.
Cath Fox	We have muted too Andy. Is that correct?
Rose Brettell	We can't hear anyone.
Emma Oldham	I think people are just chatting for now, Cath… so you'll be able to unmute for a bit, I guess.
Ann Ball	Same here. I can't hear.
Justin Scriven	Can't hear anyone either. Mute not on.
Cath Fox	All frozen on our screen!
Chris Perry	Can't hear anything and only our picture is showing?
Ann Ball	Working now, thanks Emma.
Justin Scriven	We can't hear anyone.

Trevor Lambeth.	Those who can't hear may need to unmute their pc via keyboard not just Whats App.
Rose Brettell	Neither can we.
Justin Scriven	We can only access through Kirsty's phone. Is there a separate link? We want it through the laptop.
Krish Birhah	We can hear Tim. Can't see you.
Emma Oldham	I just downloaded the zoom app Justin, and then typed the meeting id number in, and it connected.
	Sorry can't help anymore. Good luck!
Krish Birhah	I think people have decided not to show their image.
Mary Peter	I can't hear anyone, and my phone isn't muted.
Rose Brettell	Is it a different code now?
Emma Oldham	Yes Rose.
Rose Brettell	What is it please?
Chris Perry	We are the same.
Emma Oldham	I can't seem to paste it, Rose.
Justin Scriven	It won't let us in.
Trevor Lambeth	Yes code changed 857683909
Justin Scriven	This link won't let us in.
Emma Oldham	Are you using the new code, Justin?
Justin Scriven	The one above
Emma Oldham	How strange… that's the new one. Should we all be muted now?
Justin Scriven	We are in on the phone but can't open it on the laptop.
Rose Brettell	Are we supposed to be seeing Tim?
Emma Oldham	We can't for some reason.
Rose Brettell	OK we still can't hear anyone.

Cath Fox	Sorry if we are supposed to be doing something, but we don't know what to do?
Emma Oldham	Technology!
Alison Dix	Not getting any sound either. Thought it was my computer, but maybe not.
Emma Oldham	Think lots of people are struggling with the audio, Alison.
Rose Brettell	It looks like Val and Dave are singing.
Emma Oldham	They are.
Julie Ann Johnson	Yes, definitely!
Emma Oldham	Singing 'Open the eyes of our heart'.
Mary Peters	Still can't hear.
Rose Brettell	I can't hear them.
Trevor Lambeth	Is your volume up on phone or pc.
Cath Fox	Yep
Justin Scriven	I can't hear anything
Jo Strange	Really sorry everyone, but we're having many technical problems this morning. We're doing our best to get things sorted. It's working for some people but not for others. Tim is speaking now if you can hear him. Don't forget to click your start video button and unmute button. Please bear with us!
Rose Brettell	Can hear Tim
Krish Birhah	Please can we all put ourselves on mute? Thanks
Trevor Lambeth	Sound not good, Krish.
Krish Birhah	There is too much interference.

Trevor Lambeth	Whoever set this should be able to mute everyone.
Emma Oldham	But then we wouldn't hear Cath and Martin, I think Trevor.
Chris Strange	Please could you mute yourselves so it's just Martin and Cath? Neither we nor Andy W can do it. Sorry!
Trevor Lambeth	The leader can choose who to open mic usually.
Chris Strange	There's a problem with Zoom and we can't do it. Frustrating I know!
Rose Brettell	Don't worry, Jo.
Trevor Lambeth	It's brilliant though temperamental. Great job for setting up.
Emma Oldham	Thank you Tim and all!
Justin Scriven	Bless Jo, Chris and team for all your hard work. We will log off and have prayer time. See you all soon.
Trevor Lambeth	Amen
Chris Perry	Thanks Jo and Chris for all your hard work. Steve has used it quite a few times and couldn't hear or see folks. Signed off in the end.
Jo Strange	Thank you for your patience. We did have some glitches today, despite our best efforts. We'll persevere. God Bless.

Post service meditation

Mal Harris	Good to see some faces this morning. Wow! That's another first for me. Bless, dear Lord, all those

207

	involved in this morning. Technology is great when it works! Have a good week.
Hazel Hughes	It was fun. I could hear and see some faces. Thank you, Chris and Jo. Time for coffee.
Chris Strange	Hi everyone. Looks like it might have been a nationwide problem and an overload of Sunday worship made it crash! That's one theory. We'll persevere.
Val Plant	Overload of worship! That can only be a good thing. So pleased to be a part of it!
Cath Fox	Great to be part of an overload of worship.
Mal Harris	Love you all and great to be together after a fashion! Just seeing faces and hearing voices lifted my spirits.

(Here ends the Zoom Liturgy)

P.S. Somewhere, in the depths of Merry Hill, Tim was sitting, all alone, in church, staring at a blank screen, and wondering what was going on.

Back to Basics

On February 29th, 2020, I took my 90-year-old mother shopping. She had been listening to the latest news on the spread of the Corona virus and insisted we needed to stock up on hand gel. It appeared that everyone else had the same idea, as every store we visited had completed sold out! I thought to myself; "At least the message on washing hands appears to have got out and people are taking action to protect themselves."

It struck me that there are so many occasions when the solution to a problem is often to go 'back to basics.' It made me think about the basics of my faith, what are the basics when it comes to how I live out my Christian faith?

Throughout this Covid-19 crisis the two fundamentals of my faith have been prayer and the bible – they are my 'back to basics'. Proverbs 4 verses 20-23 has become a constant reminder to me about the importance of the Bible and God's word.

20 My son, pay attention to what I say;
turn your ear to my words.
21 Do not let them out of your sight,
keep them within your heart;
22 for they are life to those who find them
and health to one's whole body.
23 Above all else, guard your heart,
for everything you do flows from it.
(Proverbs 4: 20-23)

I have heard a lot over the past six months about protecting ourselves, shielding ourselves from harm. For me that protections starts with God's words and His promise. Philippians 4:6 has reminded me not to be anxious about what has been going on around us, but instead to bring all my fears and concerns to God in prayer.

Do not be anxious about anything, but in every situation, by prayer and petition, with thanksgiving, present your requests to God. (Philippians 4:6)

So when I reflect on the past 6 months looking at not only the Corona virus but also the racial injustice that has come to the fore I reflect that it should not only be in times of need that I turn back to basics, but all the time. Turning back to basics is a daily task, prayer and reading the bible – It's as simple as washing your hands!
(Andy Wynter)

Chapter 9
Good Morning, my lovely church family….

The lockdown…. as it happened

For many members of St Joseph's, WhatsApp has been a lifeline. It has carried them through lockdown. It has offered a means of communication and kept the sense of fellowship alive. How much harder this lockdown would have been, had it occurred even ten years earlier. So, to conclude the Lockdown Diaries we must allow this new literary genre to speak to us: lockdown as it happened on WhatsApp (with a little help from Facebook).

For over three months, the first words that many read each morning were: "Good Morning, my lovely church family." Hazel found words of encouragement from a variety of sources and kept our spirits alive. Just a few of her reflections are included below in this WhatsApp narrative.

March 11

I came upon this written note from Life-spring Church and thought it worth sharing:

Have you checked the news recently? Coronavirus, floods, terrorism, stock markets crashing. Terror on every side.

Those words, "terror on every side" are found in the 31st Psalm. What is significant for me is that they are followed almost immediately by these words: "my times are in your hand".

So what? Well, this means that as Charles Spurgeon so eloquently put it, "we are not waifs and strays upon the ocean of fate but are steered by infinite wisdom towards our desired haven."

God is working out His purposes in all of this seeming chaos, and it will ultimately be for the good of those who love God.

"And we know that God causes all things to work together for good to those who love God, to those who are called according to His purpose. (Romans 8:28)

So come what may, God is in charge. He is working in and through all of this. He will be glorified through it even if we can't see how. It brings me great comfort to meditate on this truth; it brings me peace when it seems the whole world wants me to run screaming for the hills!

Once again, in the words of Spurgeon, "Providence is a soft pillow for anxious heads, an anodyne for care, a grave for despair.

Remember: your times are in his hand and no terror can alter a single moment of God's plan and purpose for your life here on earth.

Amen!

(contributed by Gunter Skoppek)

March 13th
Good Morning. My lovely church family.
It's not easy, Lord, to live each day for you.
But if we should try to box you in, keep banging on the lid.
Help us to reflect the beauty of your life in our world. Amen.
(quoted by Hazel Hughes)

March 15th
St Joseph's is such a church of love. How blessed me, my future wife and children feel.
(Justin Scriven)

March 16th
The Clown Prayer
Dear Lord, thank you for calling me to share with others your precious gift of laughter.
May I never forget that it is Your gift – my privilege.
As your children are rebuked in their self-importance and cheered in their sadness,
Let me remember that your foolishness is wiser than man's wisdom.
(quoted by Hazel Hughes)

March 19th
Continued prayer for all those suffering with coronavirus, and for the medics fighting against it. Amen.
(Tracey Bennett)

Positive mind, diet, exercise and trust in God. It is strange times but together we can face this challenge with a sensible adherence, overcome it and grow. Look at the possibilities that it is opening up, as well as the

negative. It's hard, but I feel an enormous calm within, about this. I am proud to see how our young are dealing it. We can learn a lot from children.
(Justin Scriven)

March 20th

It may seem we are hanging on by our fingertips. Jesus says, "Don't worry, I have overcome the world. Trust me." Remember my lovely friends, we are children of the living God in whom Christ dwells, living in the unshakable kingdom of God.
Amen! God bless your day, whatever you are doing.
(Ann Hartnell)

I just keep getting this Bible verse coming into my mind, "It is finished". We don't need to fear anything. Amen.
(Farrah Hunter Coley)

We are all connected upon the earth through God. We don't listen and we don't look after His world...no excuses! Look at how beautiful it is and yet what we do. Within this pandemic, let us look to the beautiful heavens and see what we take for granted – a beautiful gift from our heavenly Father. Let us see…. let us…. listen! We are not indispensable. Be blessed today and take time with God and keep trusting.
(Justin Scriven)

March 21st

God is good, all the time.
All the time, God is good.
(posted by Ann Hartnell)

When all this is over, I think, in true British style, we have a cream tea afternoon at St Joseph's. In the meantime, as was sung during the war, "Let's keep the home fires burning!" God Bless.
(Justin Scriven)

Looking forward to our time of prayer and togetherness.

Lord Jesus Christ, you said to your disciples,
'I am with you always.'
Be with me today, as I offer myself to you.
Hear my prayers for others and for myself,
And keep me in your care.
(posted by Chris Strange)

Hi Pete! We've kept you in our thoughts. Hope all is OK. Hope you've brought some spaghetti back mate – you'll need it.
(David Garfield)

A very challenging time for my daughter and family. They live in North Italy and have been in full lockdown since mid-February. Not easy. I am in touch with them daily, and they are coping remarkably well.
(Peter Boneham)

May God bless our parish and our world, bringing healing to how we are being affected by this terrible virus.
(Justin Scriven)

Sunday evening 7pm: Light a candle in the window of your house. I'll be in St Joseph's Church to light our church candle. Join the Archbishop's Day of Prayer for our nation.
(Tim Eady)

March 22nd. Mothering Sunday
I am particularly conscious this morning that there will be Mums who would normally see their families today and are separated because of covid-19. I pray that they will know they are not alone and that our Lord is watching over them. May they have peace and know that they are in the thoughts of loved ones even though they may not be physically together.
(Mal Harris)

Lord, although our focus is on mothers today, I ask you to surround all the children who are separated from their mothers with your love and blessing. Thank you for this modern age which allows so many distant contacts. Amen
(Tracey Bennett)

Thank you, God, for Technology. We thoroughly enjoyed the Live Service. Well done to you all who were involved to bring the church to our homes.
(Gunter Skoppek)

I never thought I'd be saying this, but technology today is amazing when we can't meet together in person. The live streaming and the What's Ap group have been wonderful. To be able to keep in touch in this way has been fab.
(Mal Harris)

March 23rd   (Lockdown begins)
Having just watched the news, my thoughts and prayers are with all my church family.
(Mal Harris)

Prayers with you, Mal and if you could think and pray for Gemma, my sister, who's working the next three nights at A and E in New Cross, that not only can she keep our family safe, but all others and their family members as well. May God keep us safe and remind us that when we walk, we do not walk alone, and when we feel weak, He will carry us through.
(Laura Lister)

Prayers for Gemma and all other people in hospitals and likewise.
(Brenda Swatman)

With God's guidance and love we will get through this and we are all going to celebrate with cake at Adventurers. Farrah is designated cake maker.
(Laura Lister)

Abi, our daughter is a paramedic. She has just finished her 4th out of 5 consecutive 12 hour shifts. We spoke yesterday and she was so upbeat, despite everything. She talked about the overwhelming human kindness that she and all her colleagues were receiving from the public. Meals, snacks, coffees, cakes, ice-creams being dropped off at the station from which she works. When she and her crew mate stopped at a farm shop to pick up lunch, they were told they didn't need to pay. They did, but when they got back to the ambulance, food had been left on it for them. The arrival at hospitals has all improved and there are no longer patients in corridors waiting to be admitted. She has admitted suspected cases but is still very positive. The only negative was the diminishing supplies of gloves, masks, etc. But hopefully that is now resolved with extra teams dispatching. Covid-19 is an

awful virus, but with all people doing the right things and good things, we will win. Good will always win. It always has and always will.
(Caroline Sanderson)

Thank you for this message. It is good to hear of God's work through His people. At difficult times people are generally amazing in their response. Prayers for all paramedic and key workers that they will keep safe. God protect them all.
(Mal Harris)

Prayers with your daughter and all other paramedics. It's hard to believe people are moaning. The NHS are being overworked with this terrible pandemic and are being scorned for being given gifts of food. May God give them all the strength they need to keep us safe.
(Laura Lister)

I listened to Margaret Heffernan, who has written a book called "Uncharted". She spoke of how life is unpredictable however hard we as humans try to make it predictable. Thank you, God, that you are predictable and in control. Thank you that you are embracing each one of us and will comfort our anxieties if we seek you. Thank you that you will supply our daily needs and through your generosity, others may be blessed.
(Hilary Bannister)

March 24th

We want all our St Joe's kids and families to know that even though usual activities aren't taking place, we are still thinking and praying for you all - and still here to help

218

if you need us in any way we can. Lots of love and prayers ♥♥♥ ♪♪♪
(Farrah Hunter-Coley)

March 26th (First night of 'the clap' for the NHS)
Lots of us on Langley Road and Fareham Crescent also fireworks.
(Pam Teece)
We had the boys out on the doorstep.
(Farrah Hunter-Coley)
Wow! Me and Jake could hear down the road, was lovely!
(Kirsty Stokes)
Fireworks by us and all our neighbours out.
(Rose Brettell)
Lots of people out at Bellencroft Gardens too!
(Mal Harris)
Loads of people out on Swan Bank to do it. Whooping, clapping and drums.
(Emma Oldham)
Could hear other people clapping and shouting and even fireworks!
(Tracey Bennett)
And York Avenue! All very emotional.
(Julie Ann Johnson)
Worked better than I expected. Even got to wave to Mal.
(Tim Eady)
Our road too.
(Caroline Sanderson)
Many out in Woodland Road.
(Andrew Bennett)
Fireworks still going off in Finchfield – feeling the love for the NHS
(Chris Strange)

All out in Bantock Gardens
(Sarah Small)
With huge thanks to our amazing care staff. Thank you, Lord for their wonderful commitment and dedication. Amen
(Mal Harris)
Hamble Road and Colesden Walk. Out clapping, whistling, shouting, horn blowing. Thank you to NHS.
(Glennis Potts)
My daughter who is a nurse in London has just text me and said all the people in her street came out and clapped. She felt very emotional but also very blessed by the support.
(Peter Boneham)
Amazing national support.
(Rose Brettell)

March 28th

I am really struggling. I start the day refreshed and then throughout the day become more and more laden down with information and worry. Terribly anxious. And feeling so guilty for not putting my trust in the Lord to take complete control.
(Farrah Hunter Coley)

Bless you, Farrah. We are being bombarded with new information all the time, and we are only human. It's natural to respond like this initially. Try to keep on reading His Word and praying often. He loves you so very much and wants to support you every step of the way.
(Emma Oldham)

Hi Farrah, you're allowed to feel anxious as we are going through a worrying time. The Lord understands how you feel. Don't feel guilty! May the Lord wrap His arms around you today and give you strength.
(Julie Ann Johnson)

It's a testing time for all of us, especially growing families. I have just this minute read, "But God can be trusted to make you strong and protect you from harm" (2 Thess 3:3)
(Farrah Hunter Coley)

Stay strong in the Lord our God, everyone.
(Brenda Swatman)

It is such a strange time for us all. Help us, Lord, to rest in you, knowing that you are in control and will give us the strength to get through.
(Mal Harris)

March 29th
Everyone with willing hands to do God's urgent work;
Wanted: those who will not falter, quail or shirk;
Wanted: sympathetic hearts to ease the world's distress;
Wanted: helpers for the job of spreading happiness.
  -    Thought for the day for another Sunday.
(posted by Hazel Hughes)

Thank you to everyone who joined in with our ADVENTURER'S LIVE session!!!!!!! Stay safe in your ark through the storm with God by your side, the sun will eventually shine again.
(Farrah Hunter-Coley)

March 30th
Lord, at this time when everything is so uncertain, help us to remember that You and Your love are steadfast. You are the certain thing among all of the worry and confusion. Let us all look to you for certainty and for help. You are a caring Father and know exactly what we need; You meet us before we even approach you with prayer as you know all of our thoughts. Please let others who are worried and lost look to you, Lord, even if it is the first time they ever have. Help us to remember that you are working and healing all of the time; we are not alone; You are holding each one of our hands. In your loving name we pray. Amen.
(Farrah Hunter-Coley)

April 3rd
I miss Steve and Chris being in the kitchen with their warm welcome when I walk through the door. I miss Graham with his smile when he sees you are there and the way that both him and Tim are always so calm and softly spoken no matter what. Wish we could be there all together still. I always look forward to Wednesday chat with everyone.
(Trudy Robinson)

April 5th.   Palm Sunday
Prayer for the Day
Christ humbled himself and became obedient unto death, even death on a cross.
Therefore God has highly exalted him
and given him the name that is above every name.
Praise to you, O Christ, King of eternal glory.

Almighty God,
who in your tender love towards the human race
sent your Son our Saviour Jesus Christ

to take upon him our flesh and to suffer upon the cross:
grant that we may follow the example
of his patience and humility,
and also be made partakers of his resurrection;
through Jesus Christ our Lord. Amen.

April 6th

Dear Jo, so loved and missed by us all. I echo the words that various ones of you have written. I've sat and read them all and cried. Michael Hunter, Phil Cansdale, Carl Rudd all have said fitting remembrances of lovely Jo. They send love to St Jo's. Some words here that I sense Jo lived out as a faithful servant of her Lord.

"Devote yourselves to prayer, being watchful and thankful. And pray for us, too, that God may open a door for our message, so that we may proclaim the mystery of Christ, for which I am in chains. Pray that I may proclaim it clearly, as I should. Be wise in the way you act toward outsiders; make the most of every opportunity. Let your conversation be always full of grace, seasoned with salt, so that you may know how to answer everyone." (Colossians 4:2-6)

1 Timothy 2:1-2 "I urge, then, first of all, that petitions, prayers, intercession and thanksgiving be made for all people— for kings and all those in authority, that we may live peaceful and quiet lives in all godliness and holiness."

Words encourage us to pray for our leaders. Praying for Prime Minister at this time.
(Pam Teece)

(Boris was admitted to hospital today, with coronavirus).

Yes Pam, we need strong leadership during these difficult times. We pray for leaders from across the world to show strong leadership whilst showing compassion for their people. God her our prayer as this devastating virus runs wild.
(Mal Harris)

May God's love be with us all. Praying for a night of peace and rest for us all.
(Caroline Sanderson)

April 7th

Jo, my Saturday breakfasts will never be the same. Can you get pikelets where you are? The world will have to put itself right without our help now. But it's not doing too good. Just read Colossian 4:6 "The goal is to bring out the best in others in a conversation, not to put them down or cut them up." That sums up your attitude. How did you manage to not deviate from that? Just been thinking of the very many events small and large we've seen in the last 30 odd years. Not just us, but your many friends. You've left us too early.
(Brian Templar)

By the way, everybody - a special 'Thank you' to the Co-op on Warstones Road. They gave us the Easter eggs that all the Adventurers will enjoy on Easter Sunday.
(Tim Eady)

April 9th   Maundy Thursday
Prayer for the Day
Lord, in the Garden of Gethsemane,

you shared with everyone who has ever been afraid.
You conquered fear with love and returned saying, 'Do not be afraid.'
In the light of your love, death has lost its sting, and so has fear.
Lord, may your love be the key that releases me from fear. Amen.

April 10th   Good Friday

Good Morning my lovely church on this Good Friday at home.
A special prayer for Easter:
God made us aware that the Saviour died and was nailed to a cross and crucified,
not to redeem just a chosen few, but to save all who ask for forgiveness from you.
Blessings to you. Have a good day.
(Hazel Hughes)

"You went to Calvary, there you died for me.
Thank you Lord, for loving me."
(Tracy Bennett)

"Oh trampled death, where is your sting?
The angels roar for Christ the King."
(Farrah Hunter Coley)

A Prayer for the Day.

Eternal God, in the cross of Jesus
we see the cost of our sin and the depth of Your love:
in humble hope and fear may we place at His feet
all that we have and all that we are,
through Jesus Christ our Lord. Amen.

April 12th   Easter Sunday

"He is not here. He has risen."
(Sign posted on the outside door of St Joseph's Church)

He is risen indeed. Hallelujah!
(Farrah Hunter Coley)

The Lord is risen. He is risen indeed. Hallelujah!
(Mary Peters)

Isn't it amazing that our awesome God who made night and day, land and sea, planets and stars also calls us His children and invites us to call Him Father.
The promise of Easter is witnessed and heard in each budding flower and each singing bird.
For Easter and spring are God's loving way of showing us that He is still with us today.
God made us aware that the Saviour died, and was nailed to a cross and crucified, not to redeem just a few, but to save all who ask forgiveness from you.

Everywhere across the land, you see God's face and touch His hand,
For everyone who needs God's healing hand today.
Each time you look up in the sky,
Or watch the fluffy clouds drift by
Or feel the sunshine warm and bright,
Or watch the dark night turn to light,
Or hear a blue bird gaily sing,
Or see the winter turn to spring,
Or stop to pick a daffodil,
Or gather violets on some hill,
Or touch a leaf or see a tree,

It's all God whispering, 'This is me, and I am faith and I am light,
And in me there shall be no night.

Come Easter!
With your golden key.
Reveal the golden daffodil
Unlock the tulip's hard green case when the door is open wide.
We shall discover hope anew where frosts of grief have changed to dew.
That God was with us all the time,
Guiding us through frost and storm,
To Easter days and sunshine warm.
The world grows fairer because God smiles.
(quoted by Hazel Hughes)

Prayer for the Day:

Christ our Passover has been sacrificed for us:
so let us celebrate the feast, not with the old leaven of corruption and wickedness:
but with the unleavened bread of sincerity and truth. (1 Corinthians 5.7b, 8)

Christ once raised from the dead dies no more:
death has no more dominion over him.
In dying he died to sin once for all:
in living he lives to God. See yourselves therefore as dead to sin:
and alive to God in Jesus Christ our Lord. (Romans 6.9-11)

Christ has been raised from the dead: the first fruits of those who sleep.

For as by man came death: by man has come also the resurrection of the dead; for as in Adam all die: even so in Christ shall all be made alive.

April 13th
Amen. May the blood of Jesus cover us.
(Crystal Taylor)

Thinking of our lovely church family. Really missed celebrating Easter with you all.
I hope we have one 'almighty' celebration once we are gathered together again. God Bless you all.
(Justin Scriven)

April 15th
Starting the day:
It's not easy, Lord, to live each day for you,
But if we should try to box you in, keep banging on the lid. Help us to reflect the beauty of you in our life.
Prayers and blessings. Have a good day.

April 17th
Prayers for those who are not able to be with loved ones at this difficult time.
(Mal Harris)

Just a thought for Friday afternoon: two years ago we had a holiday in Japan during blossom season - absolutely beautiful, but do you know what - on a walk to do essential shopping at Warstones Road Co op, the blossom in Merry Hill is just as spectacular - no need to go anywhere else, just enjoy our environment here.
Let everything that has breath praise the Lord!
(Tim Eady)

April 21st

Good Morning my lovely church family:
We all long for heaven where God is,
But we have it in our power to be happy with him at this very moment.
Being happy with Him now means loving as he does,
Helping like he gives,
Giving as He gives, serving as he serves
Rescuing as He rescues,
Being with Him twenty-four hours a day,
Touching Him in His distressing disguise. (Mother Theresa of Calcutta)
(quoted by Hazel Hughes)

April 23rd St George's Day
Prayer for the Day

Almighty God, who gave to your servant George boldness to confess the Name of our Saviour Jesus Christ before the rulers of this world, and courage to die for this faith: Grant that we may always be ready to give a reason for the hope that is in us, and to suffer gladly for the sake of our Lord Jesus Christ; who lives and reigns with you and the Holy Spirit, one God, for ever and ever. Amen

April 26th. Prayer for the Day

To people we have yet to love, and answers we have yet to find:
Loving God, guide us and lead us.
Through challenges we have yet to face, and to courage we have yet to need: Loving God, guide us and lead us.
Through suffering we have yet to feel and pain we have yet to know:
Loving God, guide us and lead us.

In the renewing of our nation and the inspiration of new life:
Loving God, guide us and lead us.
Towards dreams we have yet to follow, and horizons we have yet to see:
Loving God, guide us and lead us.
In the freedom of hope and the promise of all creation:
Loving God, guide us and lead us.

April 30th
Good morning my lovely church family. Reassurance.
Give us reassurance when everything goes wrong, so our faith remains unfaltering and our hope and courage strong.
'Be strong and take heart, all you who hope in the Lord.' (Psalm 31:24)
Today, be a living mirror – reflect your faith in God.
(quoted by Hazel Hughes)

Thank you, Tim and Hazel. During Tim's time of prayer, three R's stood out to me:
Redemption, Reconciliation and Righteousness.
Then Hazel provided the 4th R – Reassurance.
We are redeemed through the death of Christ.
We are reconciled to God because Christ died for us.
We are to strive towards the righteousness of Christ.
We have reassurance because Christ died for us.
Thank you, Jesus.
(Tracey Bennett)

May 1st
The lockdown has affected me on some days. One day I just took myself off to bed in the middle of the day. I really

miss friends and family and the things we take for granted. I long to see the sea. Within all of this, however, I see the splendour of God's creation – the minute details and the goodness of His people....

We must place into His hands 'the things we cannot do... for I know, I always can trust you'.

(Justin Scriven)

May 2nd

I have a theory that age doesn't matter. It's attitude that's important. The oldest member of one of my congregations was 101. She had a zest for life, was alert and quick-witted and had the most lovely, unlined face. One day she said to me that she wanted to buy a new coat for winter, 'but I want a good one,' she said, 'because I want it to last!' (Paul Hulme)

(posted by Hazel Hughes)

God is saying to you right now:

"My child, you are worrying too much.

Remember who I am, there's nothing too hard for me.

You may not see it, but everything will work out in the end.

Have faith!

(Word posted by Justin Scriven)

An early morning prayer

Can you tell me what the day is? as they all seem quite the same. As I sit here, in my corner, and my tears fall like the rain. As I think of all my loved ones who seem oh, so far away. "Keep them safe from harm, dear Lord", are the words I pray. I hope they know how much I love them and that I long to kiss their face, to chat, to laugh and share good times, to feel their warm embrace. When this

time of trial is over and we meet up once again. The biggest smile upon my face, there will be no more pain.
(Tracey Bennett)

Our God is a mighty King, worthy of honour. We bow now before him in awe and in wonder that mountains and oceans and all earth's dry land are held in the palm of our Lord's holy hand.

Our God is a gracious king, full of compassion. He sent his own Son to die for our redemption. His goodness and mercy flow down from aboveAnd all that he asks in return is our love.
(Tracey Bennett)

May 3ʳᵈ
Good morning my lovely church family….
When I first crossed the Irish Sea to work in London as a lay missionary, I spent most of my days on the streets, knocking on doors and trying to help people in need. There's one door I remember in particular, because of the words written just above the letterbox: they read 'Bring good news – and knock loudly'. (Rt Revd Roy Williamson)
(quoted by Hazel Hughes)

Good Morning everyone. I hope you are all keeping safe and are in good spirits.
(Mal Harris)

Happy Sunday! As the video says, our building is closed, but the church is alive.
(Val Plant)

May 4th

"For the Lord is the Spirit and wherever the Spirit of the Lord is there is freedom (2 Corinthians 3:17)

How do you know when the Holy Spirit is present in your life? You should be able to tell by the sense of freedom you feel. If you feel oppressed, depressed or obsessed something in your life is out of kilter, seek out God's Spirit. He wants you to be free.

A Prayer:

Holy Spirit fill me with a sense of freedom only you can provide. Free my spirit from chains of oppression and draw me into the wide-open spaces of your peace. Amen.

(Posted by Mary Peters)

May 5th

Prayer for the Day

Almighty God, you have provided the resources of the world
To maintain the life of your children,
and have so ordered our life that we are dependent upon each other.
Bless us all in our daily work, and, as you have given us
the knowledge to produce plenty, so give the will
to bring it within the reach of all;
through Jesus Christ our Lord. Amen.

May 7th

PENNFIELDS PARISH -THY KINGDOM COME 2020

We are excited to be joining in with this prayer initiative between Ascension and Pentecost and will be praying continuously from 21st – 31st May 2020. Please join in with this prayer initiative by signing up to pray

(Treena Larkin)

May 8th

VE Day, pause – rather than rush. In every life there's a pause that is better than onward rush. Father help us to understand the importance of rest – for without the pause there could be no symphony. Teach us to pause more and listen for the Spirit's voice. In Christ's name.
Forget-Me-Not: Flower of friendship. Every year forget-me-nots appear around the borders, hazy blue. My long-lost friend, I think of you. These tiny flowers of May take me back to yesteryear. And walking in my garden plot, I hear you say, Forget Me Not.
(Hazel Hughes)

The following was in my mother's autograph book:
"The Maker gave a name.
Back came a little blue eyed one,
All timidly it came.
And standing by the Father's side,
It said in. accents low:
Sadly, the name Thou gavest me,
Alas! I have forgot.
Gently the Father looked it down,
And said, Forget-Me-Not."
(Caroline Sanderson)

Prayer for the 75th Anniversary of VE Day

Let us pledge ourselves anew to the service of God, and our fellow men; that we may help, encourage, and comfort others, and support those working for the relief of the needy and for the peace and welfare of all nations.
Lord God our Father, we pledge ourselves
to serve you and all mankind, in the cause of peace,

for the relief of want and suffering, and for the praise of thy name.
Guide us by thy Spirit; Give us wisdom;
Give us courage; Give us hope;
And keep us faithful, now and always. Amen.

May 9th
Prayers for all on here who are struggling.
May God pour his love and mercy onto all and into their hearts too.
May we all know of him and his unending love for us and may we feel patience during this time.
(Justin Scriven)

Amen, Justin for this prayer. I'm echoing it.
Love and God surround each one mentioned above.
(Pam Teece)

May 10th
Hi Guys! Butch here. This video was a bit of a struggle to make today – he was holding me in one hand, and his phone in the other hand. Bit worried that the visual quality doesn't do me much justice! 😟 But hey! We are back in church to film, so lots of good about it as well. 🦩
(Butch)

Father God, be with us tonight as we join together at your table. Give us hearts and ears to listen to You through Tim's spoken words. Please be with all the communications links and Jo who is working on it, and anyone else bringing you to us tonight. Amen.
(Brenda Swatman)

Thank you so much to everyone for making it possible for us to be together for communion. It was so special.
(Alison Dix)

Lovely to see so many of our wonderful church families' faces tonight on Zoom Communion.
(Emma Oldham)

Thank you, Father God for the service we just had. Thank you for sending your Holy Spirit to be with us. Lord, we thank you for providing the tech and people to lead us. Amen.
(Brenda Swatman)

I hadn't realised how much I had missed everyone until this evening.
(Val Plant)

What a surreal experience, but great to see everyone's faces. I so miss my church family.
(Mal Harris)

I'm just worshipping non-stop after communion!!!! It was lovely to see the body of Christ. Love you all.
(Crystal Taylor)

St Joe's Church together.
(Kirsty Stokes)

On Thursday, for the 7th time we clapped with our neighbours for the NHS and front line staff. At 11.00am on the 8th we all stood on our doorsteps in silence for 2 minutes in memory of all who were lost or injured in WW2. We later put up the bunting, in memory of VE Day, had our tea on our drives and waved and shouted out to all our neighbours. Community at its best, united in supporting each other, aged from 1 to 96.

In the middle of the present fears and uncertainties we need to comfort of family, friends and faith. My sister, who was an SRN was 60 on VE Day. Her son made a cake, her daughter organised a family zoom chat. Simple ideas, but so rewarding. Today, I watched a service on TV, one on my phone and bits of one on Facebook. Surreal. So many wonderful people, so many wonderful conversations, much to celebrate, but much anxiety. We don't know what our future will be, and it is at these times we need to find peace and understanding.

Praying for all those who are ill, all who are grieving and upset, all who are worried or frightened. May you find rest and peace.

(Caroline Sanderson)

May 11th

Yesterday…. Today…. And Tomorrow!
Yesterday's dead; tomorrow's unborn,
so there's nothing to fear And nothing to mourn,
for all that is past and all that has been can never return.
To be live once again – and what lies ahead
or the things that will be are still in God's hands.
So it is not up to me to live in the future.
That is God's great unknown,
For the past and the present God claims as His own.
(Quoted by Hazel Hughes)

12th May
THY KINGDOM COME
Thank you to everyone who has already booked their time to pray during the 21st-31st May. We believe the Holy Spirit will do some amazing things during this time. So please join us by booking your prayer slot
(Treena Larkin)

17th May
Jesus said suffer the little children and let them come unto me. In saying 'children' perhaps Jesus wanted us to know that he values children who are no longer children but who still see the world in a child's eyes – those of us who are stilled filled with curiosity, those open to new ideas, those who are trusting and free of fear, for of such is the kingdom of heaven. Amen.

May we see that this pause in the world God has taught us to go back to the beginning and appreciate everything we have in this glorious world He created, and may we be filled with the love and guidance he gives every day.
(Laura Lister)

May 18th
"Good friends are like stars… you don't always see them but you know they are always there."
(Quoted from a parish magazine by Hazel Hughes)

May 19th
"Difficult moments, seek God.
Quiet moments, worship God.
Painful moments, trust God.
Every moment, thank God.
(Quoted from a parish magazine by Hazel Hughes)

Our Church may be closed for the time being, but as body of Christ we are still very much serving our local community. We are available to you if you are feeling lonely and want a chat. Christ Jesus is still around to Save lives! Love and Prayers to all.
(Krish Birhah on Facebook)

May 20th

We are so excited......Only 7 more hours to go before our THY KINGDOM COME prayer initiative starts. We are praying continuously from midnight tonight until Pentecost on the 31st May. It's not too late to book your time to pray. We would love it if some people would consider filling the last 5 remaining first slots on the 30th and 31st May, LETS PRAY LIKE WE HAVE NEVER PRAYED BEFORE...………...
(Treena Larkin)

May 21st   Ascension Day
Prayer for the Day
Risen and ascended Lord Jesus,
When we are numbed by the suffering of the world,
Take us back to the deep truth
Of your power and glory,
Of your invincible Kingdom,
Of your promise of reconciliation.
In the knowledge of this truth,
Help us to bring our gaze to earth
And find the strength to go into the world,
to do your will on earth as in heaven.
To build the kingdom of God
On earth as it is in heaven. Amen

Thy Kingdom Come begins: praying for others to know Jesus is one of the most powerful things we can do. Persistent prayer brings transformation to their lives.
(Thy Kingdom Come – Archbishop Justin Welby)

May 22nd

Almighty God,
we thank you for our parish,
and ask that you will be present
in all that takes place within its boundaries.
Give wisdom to those with responsibility
for making decisions which affect our corporate life.
Inspire with your Spirit
those who care for our physical,
mental, and spiritual needs;
Grant comfort and healing to any
who are in trouble, sickness or distress;
And so direct our ways
that we may prepare ourselves
for the coming of your kingdom
and live as servants of our Living Lord,
Jesus Christ. Amen.
(Tim Eady)

Never underestimate the power of prayer
(Thy Kingdom come - Archbishop Justin Welby)

May 23rd

God of our salvation,
hope of all the ends of the earth,
Thy kingdom come.
That the world may know Jesus Christ as the Prince of Peace,
Thy kingdom come.
That we may be bold to speak the word of God

while you stretch out your hand to save,
Thy kingdom come.
That the Church may be generous in giving,
faithful in serving, bold in proclaiming,
Thy kingdom come.
That the day may come when every knee shall bow
and every tongue confess that Jesus Christ is Lord,
Thy kingdom come.

Loving God, thank you that you loved us first.
Please open my friends' eyes to your love and action for them.
(Thy Kingdom Come – Archbishop Justin Welby)

May 24th
Let us make our way together, Lord; Wherever you go, I must go:
and through whatever you pass, there too I will pass.
(Thy Kingdom Come – St Teresa of Avila)

Have you ever noticed how much of Christ's life was spent doing kind things?
(Thy Kingdom Come: Henry Drummond)

May 25th
Spent a nice hour with God this morning sitting in the sunshine. Psalm 46 verse 10 came to mind - "Be Still and know that I am God, I will be exalted among the nations, I will be exalted in the earth."
(Richard Carter TKC)

Dear Jesus dear father of mercy, I pray for this world: for the suffering, the lonely, the mentally ill, all in poverty, the alcoholics suffering addiction, the homeless, the vulnerable, that no one takes advantage of them. May they hear the birds sing; may they feel part of this world; may they find God and peace. Protect us our loving father from the worries of this world. Hold us close, protect us, keep us safe from fear, may we continually pray, Lord, to you to be your child. God bless the sick; bless the evil that they may find you, my loving Father Amen

(Daniella Brooks)

Thank you, Lord, that so many people are hearing your voice so clearly over this time. May this continue and MORE...... May each of us see MORE of you in our lives. Hear MORE of you during our prayer times and Speak MORE of your words to share our faith to the five people we are praying for. We are ready and waiting for MORE Lord.......

(Treena Larkin)

May 26th

"Every day is like a suitcase – some people pack more into it than others."

(quoted by Hazel Hughes)

"In a world of unrelenting changes, I am the one who never changes. I am the Alpha and Omega, the First and the Last, the Beginning and the End. Find in Me the stability for which you have yearned.

I have created a beautifully ordered world: one that reflected My perfection. Now, however, the world is under the bondage of sin and evil. Every person on the planet faces gaping jaws of uncertainty. The only antidote to this poisonous threat is drawing closer to Me. In My Presence you can face uncertainty with perfect Peace. *"(from a Leprosy Mission book, quoted by Mary Peters)*

May 27th
Thank you, God, for our lovely space in our community. Lord, protect and keep the area safe for us all to enjoy. Be with me now as I pray in this hour of Thy Kingdom Come.
(Brenda Swatman)

Read Psalm 100 during prayers and the passage "Come before him singing with joy" stood out for me this morning. Then Read Psalm 143 which includes "Help me to do your will for you are my God lead me in good paths for Your spirit is good".
(Mary Peters)

Prayer time today seemed to flow all day!
Special blessings from friends so thankful.
Led me to the "Job" verses: [18] You will be secure, because there is hope; you will look about you and take your rest in safety. [19] You will lie down, with no one to make you afraid, and many will court your favour.

The holy Spirit knew I needed to read these as I've been having a struggle! Thankyou Lord for hearing me. Giving all to Him I could prayer for those He is waiting to draw to himself.
(Pam Teece)

May 30th
We pray for all children returning to school this week. We pray for all of our families in Church during this time –

whether children are going back to school or staying at home. Lord protect them all
(Farrah Hunter-Coley)

During my hour of prayer last night, the first words that came into mind were "torrents of water". This didn't link with anything I had been reading or thinking. Whilst looking for a Psalm I was drawn to Psalm 117, possibly the shortest? The words, however, were quite straight to the point, mentioning God's strong love and eternal faithfulness. These words brought forth the chorus Faithful One, so unchanging. The words "all through the storm your love is the anchor" possibly linked to the earlier mentioned torrents. I saw a picture of this water washing us all with love and the Holy Spirit. Then finally my hour of prayer finished with the chorus "Peace is flowing like a river" flowing out through you and me.
(Tracey Bennett)

During my time of prayer just now my pause with God took me to the verse "Be still and know that I am God" the one who heals, and the one to trust.
I listened to "What a beautiful name"
JESUS Yours is the Kingdom.
Break every chain spoke to me too. Only He can do that.
for those he's given us to pray for that this is what He'll do. I also pray that as we celebrate Pentecost your church Lord will be Ablaze with the Holy Spirit and people dipping into these streamed times will be touched by you Lord.
(Pam Teece)

11pm Day 10 - Pennfields Parish - Thy Kingdom Come

Last 11 hours of continuous prayer. Let's dig deep into our prayers as we pray for the Holy Spirit to fall upon the 5 people we are praying for and for a transformation of the nation.

Join us by lighting a candle as we conclude our prayer time at 10am tomorrow uniting our prayers across the parish.

(Treena Larkin)

May 31st Pentecost
Prayer for the Day Pentecost
Holy Spirit give us faith
Holy Spirit give us hope
Holy Spirit give us love.
Revive your work in this land beginning with me.

June 1st
Dear Lord, this morning we pray for children, families and staff, as they return to school and things still seem a little strange and uncertain. Lord, ease anxieties. Lord, protect them, strengthen them, bless their day with calmness and happiness. We ask this in your Son's precious name. Amen.

(Farrah Hunter-Coley)

Love is still at the centre of the universe. Still available. And God, who is love, is still trying to pour it into our lives. Have a good day.

(Eddie Askew, quoted by Hazel Hughes.)

We have been on an amazing journey with God through our 250 hours of continuous prayer for Thy Kingdom Come. It has been wonderful to see how God has spoken to you all in so many amazing ways. Lets keep praying

for the 5 people that God placed on our hearts, that they will know the love of Jesus and be transformed by the Holy Spirit.
(Treena Larkin)

June 2nd
Adventuring Lord, grant us the courage to move beyond our little certainties, knowing that wherever we go, you are there, ahead of us.
(Quoted by Hazel Hughes)

June 3rd
It's approaching – my big day.
All my butterflies have fluttered away, all my glee has shone to silence and because of covid-19.
Oh covid -19 I wish I could stick a pin inside you and poke you to non-existence. You deflated my plans to get married and wedded to my chosen man.
Why covid-19? Why?
Not only have you locked down weddings, you have to go and lock down pubs too.
I have kissed. Celebrating goodbye instead of kissing my husband at the altar as a bride, in my white dress, looking and feeling ever so beautiful as I walked down the aisle with close loved ones present, and I take several steps of faith to the institution of marriage.
Now, because you have closed that door, I'm now stuck inside.
All I can do is….. well, what can I do?
I refuse to cry.
Take that covid-19!
Did you think I would be depressed?
No dress; no band; no kissing my husband.
But I'm OK covid-19 because you will have to get out of the way, and very soon.

'and this too shall pass'.
Hurry uppppp and pass. I've had enough.
Arghh!
Enough of you.
Get out of the way.
Let me out!
Enough is enough.
And you, covid-19 will not have my summer either.
No way!
I want to go out to the park, the beach, the pub, shopping.
I want my life back.
I miss shopping.
Covid-19 – I'm taking my mask off.
(Crystal Taylor)

June 7th

So, I have been challenging myself to go outside every single day for the last 21 days. It was a total drag at first and I didn't want to do it, I'd rather crawl in my shall and curl up and stay in bed. By day five I was getting into the groove and the weather helped too. By day nine I even started going out twice a day with ease. I reached day 21 and didn't stop there, I carried on, day 23, 24, 25, of fresh air and walks to get out of my shell. I'm not stuck indoors, now – yay!!
(Crystal Taylor)

Well done, Crystal! Welcome to the community of us who have to go outside every day to get their brains going properly. So proud of you! God Bless
(Val Plant)

Today, on my run, I stopped off at St Joe's. I walked up the car park to the doors that none of us have entered in months; I touched them, longing to enter them. I surveyed the windows, the corner of the church that I have stood in worship so many times, the window I have worked the sound and visual desk. I prayed that God will open up our churches soon. Never more have I felt the need to connect. We need to connect, spiritually, with Him, as one. God loves us all, for we are one.
(Justin Scriven)

June 8th
I'm freeeeee! My self isolation has officially ended.
(Dan Fox)

The Lord has indeed been good to us.
Thank you, Lord, that Dan has conquered another hurdle. Super news, Dan.
(Tracey Bennett)

'I can do all things through Christ who strengths me (Philippians 4:13)
(Crystal Taylor)

June 14th
Another Sunday! Pocket prayers! O give thanks to the Lord! Call upon His name; make known His deeds among the peoples. Sing to Him. Sing psalms to Him; talk of His wondrous works! (1 Chron 16:8-9) Help us to be a light that shines towards You this day. It is often hard for us to stand out from the world and be different. My prayers also; blessing be with you all.
(Hazel Hughes)

Great service by Zoom again, and lovely to hear great worship again. Aren't we blessed at St Jo's by the different talents of our church family? And they all said AMEN.
(Mal Harris)

My phone ran out of battery, and the iPad disconnected, so I missed it.
(Brenda Swatman)

June 15th
I lost my internet on my phone.
(Hazel Hughes)

I did catch the last bit of the zoom meeting. I felt like I was late to church. It still feels great to know that church is alive and to hear from everyone. Cheers me up, that.
(Crystal Taylor)

June 18th   (Church open for personal prayer)
How lovely it felt to have prayer in our church again, after so long, to have some connection. We pray that this will move forward and that we will slowly come together as 'one' very soon. Amen!
(Justin Scriven)

Such a powerfgul statement to see the doors open! Felt a refreshing glimmer of hope much bigger tonight as we prayed. So looking forward to the day we can all gather together once again.
(Kirsty Stokes)

Amen Kirsty! Yes a statement that church is 'open' and has persevered. Let's hope that more will be aware and

accept the invitation to enter. Definitely a right step.... 'from small acorns doth grow mighty oaks!' God will do His will.
(Justin Scriven)

June 19th
(In response to Black Lives Matters)
"Violence never brings permanent peace. It solves no social problem: it merely creates new and more complicated ones. Violence is impractical because it is a descending spiral ending in destruction for all. It is immoral because it seeks to humiliate the opponent rather than win his understanding: it seeks to annihilate rather than convert.

"Violence is immoral because it thrives on hatred rather than love. It destroys community and makes brotherhood impossible. It leaves society in monologue rather than dialogue. Violence ends up defeating itself. It creates bitterness in the survivors and brutality in the destroyers."
(Martin Luther King, during his speech when he received the Nobel Prize for Peace in 1964)
(posted by Glennis Potts)

June 20th
'There was an old owl liv'd in an oak
The more he heard, the less he spoke.
The less he spoke, the more he heard;
O, if men were all like that wise bird!

Have a good day.
(Hazel Hughes – quoted from Punch, 1975)

June 21st
"Church is home.

Church is friends.
Church is family.
You need them
They need you.
(Tracey Bennett – quoting an older post)

June 22nd

Off to the dentist. My first visit anywhere in last three months, and in another building! Prayers please.
(Pam Teece)

June 23rd

Blessed are those who can laugh at themselves, they will have endless amusement.
Blessed are those who can tell a mountain from a molehill, they will be spared a lot of trouble.
Blessed are those who are intelligent enough not to take themselves seriously, they will be appreciated by those around them.
(quoted by Hazel Hughes)

Jesus is the way, truth and light.
Jesus is not a way to God, but the only way to God.
Jesus is the way to everything I need, now and forever.
As I put my faith in Christ, I know He will be my way.
(quoted by Crystal Tayler)

July 5th

Good morning my lovely church family.
Witty item in church magazine: Come work for the Lord. The labour is intensive, the hours are long and the pay is low, but the retirement benefits are out of this world.
This is my last Thought for the Day as we are coming out of this lockdown. My prayers and blessing to you all.

(Hazel Hughes)

(First post-lockdown "open air" service held outside St Joseph's.)
What a delight to see people of all ages gathering together for the first time in over three months. To be able to bring the children again has truly blessed us.
(Justin Scriven)

So lovely to see everyone this morning.
(Ann Hartnell)

July 6th
Even though I missed the beginning of the service, it was lovely to be back with my church family. The kids loved it. It was so lovely seeing everyone. We've missed you all. I think it was lovely how the kids just got the worn-out ball. I was just so happy to be around each other. The simple things really are the best and that definitely was one good thing through this God has shown us – to appreciate the little things and how beautiful our world is.
I'm so glad Steve unknowingly brought me back to church and with you all. The piece of puzzle missing in my life was God, and you all.
(Laura Lister)

Amen, and Amen!

Epilogue

The lockdown has continued for much longer than most of us expected. Back in March, I rather naively anticipated that we would have a few weeks of peace and quiet, and then, suddenly, with a bang, everything would start up again. It hasn't quite been like that.

At the time of writing, we are slowly moving out of lockdown; we can now hold small services in church, as long as we keep our distance from each other, and wear our masks. People are beginning to ask about resuming normal activities. But there is still a long way to go. Singing in public is strictly forbidden, and the threat of increased lockdown is constantly held over us.

So what is the new 'normal'? We are still learning and finding out.

What lessons have we learned through lockdown? Just a few thoughts:

Slow down. It is sometimes said, 'there's a reason why we are called human beings, and not human doings.' So often, it seems as if we are measured by what we do. These months of lockdown have obliged all of us to learn the importance of simply 'being' – being the people we are intended to be. So a lockdown resolution – discover your inner self.

Appreciate what we have. Two years ago, I had the privilege of a holiday in Japan during blossom season. It was stunningly beautiful. But I learned this year – the spring blossom on the Warstones Estate is just as good. I arrived in Wolverhampton last year with every intention of some good days out in Shropshire – walking the Wrekin and the Long Mynd. Instead, I have discovered the myriad footpaths around Merry Hill, I've been along the railway path and the canal towpath. They're beautiful. I have been forced to slow down and to appreciate what is right in front of me, and it's been good.

Look for the good in people around you. The lockdown months have been a trial, and it is distressing to see an increase in litter in our parks and unnecessary speeding on the roads, but the lockdown has brought out the good in so many ways: new friendships with neighbours; spontaneous caring and support for one another; appreciating what other people do for us.

Faith is for real. So often, it is only when we are stripped of all the regular activities that take up our time that we have time to discover that God is with us. Our faith in the God who created us, redeemed us and fills us with His grace and power, is a solid rock upon which we can build our lives.

And we have hope. Hope for a future. Covid-19 will not have the last word.

My help comes from the Lord, the Maker of heaven and earth. (Psalm 121:2)

As people who trust in God's promises. We know that there is a future. The problems of this transitory life are but for a season. God promises will endure for ever. So we look to the future, ready and committed to serve God, and bring His new life to all who will believe.

The steadfast love of the Lord never ceases, his mercies never come to an end;
they are new every morning; great is your faithfulness.
(Lamentations 3: 22 – 23)

Acknowledgements

Over 100 people contributed to this collection. My sincere thanks to all of them. The majority are the present-day saints of St Joseph's Church. However, these months of 'lockdown' have provided the opportunity for members to rediscover old documents, including letters, magazines, minute books, and photos (which merit their own exhibition) and have enabled some of the 'saints in glory' to have their writings included.

The end result provides a rich tapestry of life and ministry, past and present, at St Joseph's.

The original history of St Joseph's was written in 1983 by Don Bannister, and his work has been essential reading for St Joseph's historians ever since. With his permission, some of his original work is used here.

Special thanks to the former ministers of St Joe's, who have shared their own memories, especially David Banting through whose ministry the 'new' St Joseph's Church was built, and whose enthusiasm shines through in all that he has written, in both his lockdown letter, and the many original documents which derive from him.

What a pleasure it has been to share in this project with so many committed people!